Finding Jesus
in the Psalms

**Finding Jesus in the Psalms:
A Lenten Journey**

Finding Jesus in the Psalms
978-1-7910-2674-5
978-1-7910-2675-2 *eBook*

Finding Jesus in the Psalms: DVD
978-1-7910-2678-3

Finding Jesus in the Psalms: Leader Guide
978-1-7910-2676-9
978-1-7910-2677-6 *eBook*

BARB ROOSE

FINDING
JESUS
IN THE
PSALMS

A Lenten Journey

Abingdon Press | Nashville

**Finding Jesus in the Psalms:
A Lenten Journey**

Copyright © 2022 Barb Roose
All rights reserved.

No part of this work may be reproduced or transmitted in any form or by any means, electronic or mechanical, including photocopying and recording, or by any information storage or retrieval system, except as may be expressly permitted by the 1976 Copyright Act, the 1998 Digital Millennium Copyright Act, or in writing from the publisher. Requests for permission can be addressed to Rights and Permissions, The United Methodist Publishing House, 810 12th Avenue South, Nashville, TN 37203 or emailed to permissions@abingdonpress.com.

Library of Congress Control Number: 2022946125
978-1-7910-2674-5

Scripture quotations are taken from the Holy Bible, New Living Translation, copyright ©1996, 2004, 2015 by Tyndale House Foundation. Used by permission of Tyndale House Publishers, Inc., Carol Stream, Illinois 60188. All rights reserved.

Scripture quotations noted CEB are taken from the Common English Bible, copyright ©2011 by Common English Bible, Nashville, Tennessee. Used by permission. All rights reserved.

Scripture quotations noted ESV are taken from the ESV® Bible (The Holy Bible, English Standard Version®), copyright ©2001, by Crossway, a publishing ministry of Good News Publishers. Used by permission. All rights reserved.

Scripture quotations marked NIV are taken from the Holy Bible, New International Version®, copyright ©1973, 1978, 1984, 2011 by Biblica, Inc.™ Used by permission of Zondervan. All rights reserved worldwide.

Scripture quotations taken from THE MESSAGE. Copyright ©1993, 1994, 1995, 1996, 2000, 2001, 2002. Used by permission of NavPress Publishing Group. All rights reserved.

Scripture quotations marked (KJV) are taken from The Authorized (King James) Version. Rights in the Authorized Version in the United Kingdom are vested in the Crown. Reproduced by permission of the Crown's patentee, Cambridge University Press.

MANUFACTURED IN THE UNITED STATES OF AMERICA

To my mom, Regina.

Thank you for teaching me about Jesus during my childhood and sparking a lifetime of learning, curiosity, and purpose.

CONTENTS

Introduction IX

Chapter One: Why Do We Need to Find Jesus in the Psalms?
　　　　　Psalm 2, Romans 8 1

Chapter Two: Finding Jesus with Us in Our Hard Places:
　　　　　Psalm 16 23

Chapter Three: Finding Jesus as Our Shepherd:
　　　　　Psalm 23; John 10:1-18 47

Chapter Four: Finding Jesus as Our Hope:
　　　　　Psalm 110, Psalm 100, Hebrews 7 71

Chapter Five: Finding Jesus as Our Strength:
　　　　　Psalm 69, Matthew 26, John 18 95

Chapter Six: Finding Jesus as Our Savior:
　　　　　Psalm 22, Matthew 27, John 20 117

Conclusion 141

Notes 143

INTRODUCTION

In our Christian journey, part of trusting God comes as a result of knowing that God is consistent in both character and love. In a world where it's hard for us to trust in anything, perhaps taking time to examine how God's steady hand has guided our human experience back to God despite our mistakes is the comforting reassurance that we need to trust him with our lives and our eternity. In this Lenten experience, we will explore God's words and guidance in the Psalms and find the presence of Jesus as we journey toward the cross.

I don't know about you, but I like to know how the pieces of life fit together, especially when I'm looking at a complicated problem. When someone gives me directions, I need to know more than "Just look for the white mailbox on the left." I like knowing what comes before and after; otherwise, my mind will fill in the blanks with my best guess and that doesn't ever turn out well.

All the big existential questions that we ask, such as figuring out the meaning of life, finding our purpose, as well as how to handle pain and suffering, can be confusing when we try to navigate them on our own. Yet, God has provided a framework and a source of support and guidance to help us to navigate those questions and experience peace along the journey. I like to call this framework "God's Big Picture." When we understand our lives from God's perspective, we find not only meaning, but hope for whatever circumstances that we're facing in life. Without understanding God's Big Picture, we're at risk of interpreting our

Introduction

pasts, our problems, or our pain in a way that isn't always healthy for our hearts. Without God's Big Picture, it's easy to wonder is anything worth it.

Long ago God knew our greatest need—your greatest need—and put a plan into place to make sure that you had access to hope and help long before the day that you were born. Discovering this is what I've enjoyed about creating this Lenten journey through the Book of Psalms.

In this study experience, we will specifically look at six chapters in the Psalms that pointedly identify a Savior, a Messiah, or a coming King. Here is an overview of the psalms and the themes that you'll explore:

1. Psalm 2: Why Do We Need to Find Jesus in the Psalms?
2. Psalm 16: Finding Jesus with Us in Our Hard Places
3. Psalm 23: Finding Jesus as Our Shepherd
4. Psalm 110: Finding Jesus as Our Hope
5. Psalm 69: Finding Jesus as Our Strength
6. Psalm 22: Finding Jesus as Our Savior

Each of these psalms were chosen because they allude to the Messiah and they highlight Lenten themes that you may be focusing on this season like worship, hope, prayer, confession, forgiveness, courage, and faith. These themes may receive extra attention during Lent, but they are excellent topics to explore at any time.

One of the intriguing features of this study revolves around the multiple layers of discovery. Even as the Psalms reveal Jesus, the same Psalms also reference King David, the author of approximately half of the Book of Psalms and considered to be Israel's greatest king. We will look at portions of King David's life that point to more about Jesus.

However, we do need divine guidance to understand what we are reading. God provides the revelation of his Word to believers who are on a journey to seek God. It's God who reveals the wisdom of the scriptures to us, but we can get ourselves into position to receive. There are three practical tools that we can use. These tools also equip us to avoid the trap of limiting our experience of the Psalms to either our modern, first-world perspective or religiosity.

Here are the three tools that you can keep in mind as you read:

- **Context:** Detailing the big picture of the scripture including who is writing along with the audience, setting, and what message is being communicated in that moment.
- **Connection:** Understanding and applying how scripture confirms itself through either relationship, symbols, or prophecy connections.
- **Jesus-Glasses:** Looking for how the passage directly references or alludes to Jesus and how that impacts our perspective.

Finding Jesus in the Psalms isn't a game of hide-and-go-seek. God didn't lead the scriptural authors in the Book of Psalms to take us on a wild hunt to find Jesus peeking at us in one verse and then hiding in the next. Rather, God's intention is for us to see and understand how Jesus spans our human history so that when we're looking at questions with no earthly answers, we can see the divine truth in Christ, his power, but most of all his love for you and me. In this Lenten journey, we find the presence of Christ in the ancient scriptures and the words that were on his lips as he moved toward the cross. The Psalms provide a perfect framework for experiencing Lent through the verses that were Jesus's own scriptures, offering both him and us strength and wisdom in a painful and redemptive season.

CHAPTER ONE

Why Do We Need to Find Jesus in the Psalms?

CHAPTER ONE
Why Do We Need to Find Jesus in the Psalms?

> *Scripture Reading:*
> *Psalm 2, Romans 8*

What is your earliest memory of Jesus?

For me, it's the memory of seeing a bronzed form of Jesus hanging on the wooden cross that was mounted on the wood paneled wall of the black Baptist church that I attended as a child. His head was down with stringy hair fallen forward and frozen in place. Even now, I'm unsure if the sculptor formed the image visualizing an alive Jesus barely clinging to life or a no longer living Jesus, fully crucified. Either way, I'm not sure if the adults around me considered how jarring it is for a little kid to repeatedly see a sized-down replica of a bronze, emaciated man with his head down wearing a sagging towel with arms stretched out, legs crossed, and glued to a piece of wood? The adults in my church passed by the Jesus-on-the-cross and carried on with business as usual, but as a kid, I had questions. Since there wasn't children's church back then, I sat in the adult service and heard the boom of the pastor's voice, "Come to the cross. Give your heart and life to Jesus," while he pointed at the large cross behind him. While I loved the stories that my mother used to teach about Jesus with the little kids, I wasn't sure about giving my heart to the inanimate man suspended on wood because what if I ended up on a cross like that? No, thank you, pastor. Another more practical concern about the Jesus-plaque: What was keeping that little slip of cloth clinging to his waist? I didn't see any safety pins or belts. It didn't seem quite right that half-naked forms of Jesus were hanging up everywhere. Sure, I'd find out later that his clothes were gambled away, but as a little kid, I didn't have context and without context, I was confused.

How often are our earliest memories of Jesus summed up with little snapshots that come from either a memory, distorted or real, from church or a snippet of a Bible story? If you were raised in church or attend regularly, much of what we learn about Jesus starts in the New Testament, beginning with the Christmas story and ending around Easter with Jesus's crucifixion and resurrection. For those who fancy themselves a little more biblically familiar, you're aware of various references to Jesus spread around the Old Testament by various people at different times. However, since we don't see Jesus mentioned by name in the Old Testament, could it be possible that we're overlooking or even missing a powerful piece, maybe even we could say *peace*, to our faith? Without understanding God's complete plan concerning Christ, it's easy for us to be confused, especially when life is uncertain or you're carrying hard questions about God without answers.

We're familiar with God as a central figure in the Bible and yes, we consider Jesus to be just as important. However, since we see God's name in the Old and New Testaments, it wouldn't be a surprise to find out that people give God more attention. Yet, what if Jesus was just as prominent in the Old Testament as the New Testament? That maybe a fresh new thought for some of you. Hundreds of prophecies were given about Jesus before he came to earth, including various allusions, symbols, and metaphoric language about Jesus that many of us have missed. There's a solid reference to Jesus in the Old Testament that points beyond the story of the Israelites' struggles and can help us better understand the heart of God.

For as long as humans have walked on earth, we've tried to figure out God. As much as God has revealed himself to humanity through creation (Psalm 19:1), his love (John 3:16), and his Word (2 Timothy 3:16-17), humans have misunderstood the heart of God, especially when we're in pain. As believers, we're not immune to those hard heart questions when our lives clash with the wages of sin that pay back all kinds of death to humanity.

Even now, there are hard questions about our fallen world that often rattle the faithful. Why doesn't God fix this? Why do bad things happen to good people? Why is life so hard? Does God even care about what I'm going through? Can God possibly love me even though I have done something wrong?

Perhaps this list of questions stirred up others for you. While I can't promise that this Lenten study experience will offer satisfactory answers to all your questions, I can promise that you'll take a journey to see and know that Jesus is our hope amid those questions. Of course, dropping the "Jesus Cares" on these hard questions isn't taking the easy way out. If you've asked one or more of these questions, I want you to know that God saw your heart, your hurt, and your confusion. Even now, God sees the battle that you may be waging just to hold onto the short string of faith that you've got left because religion hasn't helped—or religion has hurt you enough to drive you away.

In this day and time, there are a lot of people who are critical of God because their concept of God hasn't held up to the realities of their lives. Pain and disappointment scream louder than a two-year-old that wants a cookie. Perhaps even you have felt like God has taken away or kept your cookie from you, whether it was an answer to your prayer, or an answer for why he allowed something to happen.

What's interesting is that as much as our world has changed, God has not. He is not oblivious to our problems, nor is he caught off guard by our struggles. He knows our questions, our frustrations, our disappointments, and our longing and his response is and always has been the same: Jesus. While the Bible is filled with lots of stories about fascinating people, supernatural events, and puzzling interactions between God and creation, the story of the scriptures is about Jesus. When we forget that, we not only forfeit the riches of wisdom and understanding that God promises us as believers (Romans 11:33) but we also lose out on experiencing God's blessings and promises in our life right here and right now.

God is a proactive, not a reactive God. His Big Picture has always included Jesus as the solution for every stage of human history, every culture, every generation, every family, and every person, including you. Yet, we tend to include Jesus only when it's convenient for us.

For almost fourteen years, I worked on staff at my local church. If your church is anything like mine, you know that the two church services with the highest attendance are Christmas Eve and Easter Sunday. While church attendance trends have declined over the decades, those two dates stir up our religious roots, even those with dormant or nearly dead roots. We've even got nicknames for the fringe-faithful like "C&Eers" and "Chreasters." If you can, double down for a moment on any religious guilt that might be arising. This discussion isn't about how often you do or don't go to church. Rather, the big picture of this discussion is how we've limited Jesus to our human confines and whether our imposed limitations have served us well.

This elevates a crucial question: *When we limit Jesus in our heart, mind, or life, what could we be losing?*

What's So Special About the Book of Psalms?

What's the first thing that you think of when someone mentions the Book of Psalms?

Why Do We Need to Find Jesus in the Psalms?

Classified as a book of poetry, the Psalms is a collection of songs and prayers written to God. If you've got your thinking cap on, you might be wondering, "Why poetry?" Poetry is a way of "making patterns that put emotions into words."[1] If you're familiar with the Psalms, you'll know that there are a lot of emotional expressions: love, anguish, pleading, and thanksgiving expressed with visual words that connect with our heart as much as we comprehend with our heads. The Psalms were written by kings and prophets such as Moses from around the fifteen century BCE to the prophets after the Jewish people returned from exile around the sixth century BCE.[2] While centuries have passed since the Psalms were written, they are still popular today. The Book of Psalms hums with the heartbeat of our humanity with divinely inspired words that find purchase in the tenderest places in our hearts when our human words or wisdom fails us.

The Book of Psalms hums with the heartbeat of our humanity with divinely inspired words that find purchase in the tenderest places in our hearts when our human words or wisdom fails us.

How many hymns and popular worship songs have been inspired by the psalms' powerful imagery and symbolism? Here are a few notable popular verses that perhaps you've gravitated toward at certain times in life:

> *The LORD is my light and my salvation—*
> *so why should I be afraid?*
> *The LORD is my fortress, protecting me from danger,*
> *so why should I tremble?*
> (Psalm 27:1)

> *Yet I am confident I will see the LORD's goodness*
> *while I am here in the land of the living.*
> (Psalm 27:13)

> *The LORD is close to the brokenhearted;*
> *he rescues those whose spirits are crushed.*
> *(Psalm 34:18)*

> *Be still and know that I am God!*
> *(Psalm 46:10)*

Can you recall times in your life when one or more of those verses reached you when no one else could? There's something about the how the words in the Book of Psalms convey emotion around our human experience that connects our hearts with God in meaningful ways.

One of the main Spirit-led authors of the Book of Psalms is King David, who is credited with writing approximately half of the 150 psalms. Scholars debate the authorship totals of the other writers, but most will concede that David wrote at least 73 psalms.[3] Other writers include David's son, Solomon, the sons of Korah, whose ancestor was swallowed up by the earth in a great rebellion against God (Numbers 16) as well as one psalm attributed to Moses (Psalm 90). Known as the longest book in the Bible, Psalms also has the most contributors, a fact that will increase in meaning as we examine the purpose of the Book of Psalms.

Throughout our experience in the Psalms, we will see how David's writings position him as both a prophetic voice as well as a type of symbolic figure pointing to Jesus. There are several other psalms tagged as messianic or pointing to Jesus, but the ones written by David contain images and words that both overlap and connect his life and legacy to Jesus. David's poetic words spring from his warrior heart. He's a warrior poet, two words that aren't usually put together. We know that David learned how to fight as a young boy. We read about how he killed bears and lions (1 Samuel 17:36) and later Goliath (1 Samuel 17:49-50). Later, David led the Israelites into battle with such prowess that Saul was moved to jealousy when songs about David's achievements were sung in his honor (1 Samuel 18:7). Not only that, but David wasn't always reclining on a chaise lounge lingering over poetic imagery or words. He wrote from his palace, but also on the run, in a cave as well as in emotional pits and from seasons of deep grief and distance from God.

As scripture is divinely inspired, I wonder what it would have been like for David to sense that first impression from God to write poetry and songs. One wonders if the roots of David's poetry reached back into his childhood. Maybe he made up rhymes while watching his father's sheep. If you recall from some of the dialogue when David showed up to fight Goliath, his brothers would have likely teased him if he'd tried to repeat any of those poems at mealtime about the other soldiers.

One of the most direct connections is found in a title given to Jesus that's directly tied to David. There are numerous mentions of Jesus as the "son of David" in the New Testament, mostly mentioned in Matthew's account of the gospel.[4] The first time that the name "Jesus" appears in what we associate as our modern-day scriptures occurs in the first line of the Gospel of Matthew. This translation reads as follows: "This is the genealogy of Jesus the Messiah the son of David, the son of Abraham" (Matthew 1:1 NIV). This moniker was a messianic title referring to a covenant promise that God made to King David in 2 Samuel 7.

After years of running from King Saul, David finally ascends to the throne as king of Israel. Later, after he establishes Jerusalem as God's holy city for the people of Israel and hosts a massive celebration, David moves into his palace, but is troubled that the ark of the Covenant, the earthly representation of God's presence, was still housed in a tent. David expresses his desire to build a temple for God. However, the prophet Nathan comes to him after hearing from God in a dream and lets David know that God doesn't need him to build a temple. Furthermore, David isn't to be the one to build the temple because he's shed much blood on the battlefield and later, David will run into some other personal challenges.

Regardless of David's personal struggles, God enters a covenant with David, making an eternal promise to him: "Your house and your kingdom will continue before me for all time and your throne will be secure forever" (2 Samuel 7:16).

In fact, this event is retold in Psalm 132, even though scholars haven't identified the author, nor the date written with certainty.[5] This psalm reflects on David's difficult life, his desire to build a temple for the LORD, and God's promise to continue David's royal line forever, which is a reference directly to Christ.

While David wasn't chosen to build a physical temple for God, one source points out that David was the primary architect of the Psalms as a "literary temple" for God.[6] Just as David wanted to build a holy temple where people could come and worship God within literal walls, the collection of the Book of Psalms is constructed by multiple authors into a temple of worship words, offering an opportunity for not only the Israelites, but us, a way to worship God with words, but without the requirement to show up at a certain time or place or to worship God in a certain way.

As believers, we are the temple of God's Holy Spirit (1 Corinthians 6:19-20) which means that as we interact with the Psalms and as God's Words inhabit our bodies, we are human temples of worship for God. Since the Psalms are a collection of prayers, songs, and poetry, there are so many creative ways for us to connect with God according to our own unique preferences and seasons of life. In many ways, David's desire to create a lyrical house of worship and praises to God can provide inspiration for us to follow.

You can invite God to fill the space in your heart when you long for whatever you give up following him. *That's an act of worship.*

You can invite God to remind you of his faithfulness to you. *That's an act of worship.*

You can give thanks to God for his blessings. *That's an act of worship.*

These are all moments where you can be like King David and offer words that connect you with God and allow you to receive from him.

So back to the question, what's so special about the Book of Psalms? Since King David is the author of so many various psalms and he records words and imagery that speak to Christ centuries before Jesus came to earth, the Psalms remind us of God's heart for humanity, especially his intention to offer us unconditional love, grace, and salvation. Not only that, but since he represents an early type of Christ, we'll look at David's life through the lenses of the psalms. You'll get to toggle back and forth between David's life and Jesus's life and explore the unique comparisons and contrasts between David, who was called a "man after God's own heart" (1 Samuel 13:14), and Jesus, who came to earth as a man to show us God's heart.

Why Do We Need to Find Jesus in the Psalms?

From the beginning of the scriptures in Genesis through the final pages of Revelation, Jesus is God's answer to our greatest questions and the path to hope, peace, and redemption through our greatest pain. While pain and problems are the unwanted barnacles that cling to our human history, Jesus is a nail-scarred vessel carrying you through the unfair, unthinkable, unbearable things that you or others you know have gone through. Jesus may not be the answer that you're looking for, but God knows that he is the answer that you need.

Just as we do not want to evaluate the Bible based on just the Old Testament or just the New Testament, neither do we want to look at any portion of the Bible without asking, "How is what I'm reading tied to Christ?" Even beginning in the first verse of the Bible, we know that God created the world, but Jesus was present as well. John 1:2-4 explains that Jesus existed in the beginning with God as well as God created everything through Christ, concluding with this hope-filled revelation about Jesus: "And his life brought light to everyone" (John 1:4).

Jesus's presence is more than just the thirty-three years of his life on earth; rather our experience in Psalms is a reminder of what John Ortberg refers to as the "everywhereness of God."[7]

So, one of the most dangerous errors we can make in reading the Bible or reflecting on the character of God is applying any limits to our personal experience, our political or social views, or even the country that we live in. Yet, when we remember the everywhereness of Christ at all stages and seasons of human history, our faith and our hope are strengthened and grow, even as the uncertainty and anxiety of this world grow as well.

In both dramatic and unassuming places, the hope of Christ is never far from desperation or depravity of humanity.

We're now going to step into the first of six messianic psalms that not only point us to Jesus, but also illuminate the consistency of God's character, the completeness of God's plan for humanity, and his commitment to loving and caring for his children.

Psalm 2:
What's the World Going Mad About?

Why are the nations so angry?
Why do they waste their time with futile plans?
(Psalm 2:1)

Is our world going mad? It can feel like it, right? Yet, the world's been turning in chaos for a long time; it's just that we're presently on earth right now and we can hear the groaning of our planet and humanity (Romans 8:22) up close and it feels oh-so-personal. At the time that I'm writing, our country has experienced two devastating mass shootings at a grocery store in Buffalo and at an elementary school in Texas killing scores of innocent young children and adults. There's currently a war overseas, but that's really nothing new, is it? Even as the implications look dire in our present world context, the geographical lines in that part of the world have moved many times over throughout the centuries.

Why Do We Need to Find Jesus in the Psalms?

There's no dismissiveness, callousness, or even mild sarcasm in this observation, only that what we're seeing makes us nervous, but is not new to humanity.

It's at this point that we circle back to the hard questions introduced earlier such as why God doesn't intervene and stop evil or why people in power seem to get away with so much. Some are convinced that God is ignoring the cycles of pain and suffering, and others are afraid that God isn't ignoring it, but that he simply doesn't care. A small contingent also believes that we deserve whatever horror falls upon us because God is punishing us. Who's right here?

Psalm 2 relays a message that can be summed up into the following two words: "God Wins." David writes that God will send a future eternal king who will destroy every standing kingdom. Since God isn't all-smoke-no-fire, what he says will happen, even if the timeline is unknown. Of course, this ruffles our human tail feathers because we'd like to know when the bad guys are going to get it. Rather, we should concentrate on remembering that our goal is to be the light and love of Jesus rather than standing on the sidelines waiting for the world to get a whammy in the end.

As we'll see in this chapter, God has never lost control of our world, even if it seems like evil or those with evil influence dance without accountability for their actions.

The psalm opens with two questions that ring with chilling application to our world today. I've paraphrased them here: *What's everyone so mad about? Why does everyone think that they have the right answer, but they don't?*

These are two questions that could drop seamlessly into any time in human history and people would nod their heads. Just as David's son Solomon would write years later that history keeps repeating itself and, in fact, there is nothing new under the sun (Ecclesiastes 1:9). For as long as humans have inhabited the earth, we've been under the impression that our continued advancements in technology and improving our quality of life somehow mean that we've gotten smarter when it comes to existential or spiritual matters.

Years ago, I read a memoir written by NASA astronaut Leland Melvin. He was the first person in history to catch a pass in the NFL and in space. This was his observation:

> On one hand, we possessed the technical savvy to create vehicles and satellites capable of reaching distant regions of the heavens. On the other hand, we still haven't figured out the solutions to some very basic questions on Earth, such as how to keep every one of God's children safe, fed, and warm.[8]

Before Leland Melvin's comment ends up creating a rabbit trail into politics or any other related trigger topic, the point here is that as humans, we've gotten some things right as we've continued around the sun, but what we've gotten wrong hasn't changed much from the garden of Eden.

We've got this DNA-deep, dogged determination to live without relying upon God. By we, I'm including myself as well. So many times in my life, I've been convinced that my way was the right way, and down the road, I discovered that I was dead wrong. Not the kind of wrong where I read my GPS incorrectly and got lost, but the kind of wrong where I damaged a relationship or destroyed my mental health for a season. Perhaps you're thinking of your own moment in the sun when you got burned by your own brilliance. King Solomon's haunting reflection is still true centuries later: "There is a path before each person that seems right, / but it ends in death" (Proverbs 14:12).

Our plotting to live apart from God is the heart flaw in our humanity that connects us right back to the black moment in the garden of Eden. This was the dark moment when Adam and Eve became convinced that intelligence and information were more important than trusting in the sovereign wisdom of a Holy God (Genesis 3:6).

Why Do We Need to Find Jesus in the Psalms?

While Adam and Eve could have eaten from the Tree of Life, which wasn't forbidden, they shuffled right on over to what God asked them to avoid for their own good. We've lived in the shadow of that dark moment, and we've experienced its consequences of suffering, but not without hope. Yet, I wonder if we still eat from the beautiful fruit from that forbidden tree whenever we pursue, consume, or obsess about whatever sparkles, seduces, or shines apart from God? It's a heavy reflection for sure, but perhaps you can see the connection between Adam and Eve's actions and the questions asked in Psalm 2.

Who is asking these questions? If you've read Psalm 2, you know that it covers a variety of perspectives from the author asking questions to God's declaration of a savior before returning to the author who issues a warning to the world. While Psalm 2 doesn't list an author, we find out in Acts 4:25-26 that David was the author of the psalm as early church leaders Peter and John affirmed this as they taught about Jesus's resurrection.

Turns out, Jesus coming back from the dead wasn't a popular talking point for some of the listeners. This was a hot topic that riled up the Sadducees, Jewish religious leaders who were very much against that teaching. The religious leaders tossed Peter and John into jail overnight. After significant debate, the religious leaders let the men go, mainly because the numbers of believers had grown to a reported 5,000 men (and likely significant numbers of women) and the religious leaders were concerned about a riot.

After their release, Peter and John returned to the believers. It's here that they prayed and repeated David's words in Psalm 2:1:

> *You spoke long ago by the Holy Spirit through our ancestor*
> *David, your servant, saying,*
>
> > *"Why were the nations so angry?*
> > > *Why did they waste their time with futile plans?*
> > *The kings of the earth prepared for battle;*
> > > *the rulers gathered together*

> *against the LORD and*
> *against his Messiah."*
>
> *(Acts of the Apostles 4:25-26)*

I wonder if David knew the answer to the questions or if he was genuinely puzzled. To be clear, God isn't asking these questions. God is well acquainted with our human shenanigans. Not only did God watch as the people of the world gathered to build the tower of Babel planning a heaven-scraping edifice for their own purposes and desires, but he watches us build our own personal towers of Babel in our hearts and lives each day.

David notes that it isn't just individuals who are banding together against God. Rather, he cites the rulers of the world, who defend their borders against each other, but band together against God. They're willing to overlook their hatred for their neighbor because after all, the enemy of their enemy is, by default, their friend.

The result of the kings' and rulers' effort isn't shrouded in secret. They band together, even though they have no control over their own life and breath, on a mission against God and, as David points out, God's anointed one. Some translations capitalize "Anointed." No matter capitalized or not, this is a direct reference to Christ. It's not enough that the world plots against God, but Jesus is in their crosshairs as well. But why?

With bold language, their goal is declared in Psalm 2:3: "Let us break their chains and free ourselves from slavery to God."

Interesting. So, just how are they defining their enslavement to God?

The Message translation communicates verse 3 as, "Let's get free from God!" One writer points out that the same words used to describe breaking the chains and escaping slavery are like the words used to describe how God rescued the Israelites from their enemies.[9] Another source substitutes the word "yoke" for what is broken.[10] Perhaps Jesus's words in Matthew 11:30 came to mind as he describes his yoke or his teachings as relational and light. As

Why Do We Need to Find Jesus in the Psalms?

believers, we get to experience a relational connection to Christ without all the religious restrictions and rules attached by humans. However, humanity has always seemed to be more interested in doing things our way while dodging God or insisting that he get out of our way.

I was listening to a pastor who shared a story about a French revolutionary who climbed to the top of Notre Dame Cathedral to tear down the cross in hopes of symbolizing the end of the authority of God. The pastor chuckled as he finished the story: "Someone shouted back at the crowd, 'You'll have to pull the very stars from the heavens.'"[11]

In our first-world culture, we may not have the same stature as kings and rulers, but we've got enough sophistication and audacity to believe that we're the captains of our own destiny, ignoring the fact that we live by God's daily grace of fresh oxygen, clean water, and a sunrise and sunset each day.

Of course, we can declare ourselves free from God, whether we say it or not, but does that make us free? Is a fish free when someone pulls it out of the water? When I was a kid, I loved watermelon. My grandmother used to cut a big slice for me whenever I came to visit. I adored the soft fruit and sweet juice, so I begged my grandma for more. She'd tell me that one piece was enough because she didn't want to ruin my appetite for dinner. But one day, I remember that Grandma let me eat as much watermelon as I wanted. She cut the slices and sent me outside with each one on a plate so that I could spit the seeds out into the yard. I ate slice after slice. It was glorious. Until it wasn't. What felt like freedom ended up not feeling so good after all.

Later in life, I thought that I needed freedom from all of God's rules. I spent years thinking of God perched atop a giant court bench with a giant hammer. I figured that he had one bulging eye locked on me, just waiting for me to break one of his gazillion rules so that God could, as they said in my traditional Baptist church language, "smite" me. Therefore, when I had an opportunity to decide how I wanted to live away from the watchful eyes of my parents and church, I took the fast path away from God, convinced that his rules were keeping me from stuff that I wanted to see. Like Adam and Eve, I mistook God's gentle guidance to keep my heart whole and my soul unshattered for rules designed to limit my access to unlimited human experiences. I believed that I was grabbing my freedom, only to discover that far from God, I'd ended up in the grip of shame, regret, and fear.

How many of us have mistaken living any way that we wanted to for freedom? We don't think that a fish is being robbed of living its best life because it's bound inside of an aquarium of four walls. Neither are we robbed of the best of life just because God gives us guidance on the guardrails of holiness that not only protect us but keep us in his perfect peace.

Anything in excess apart from God always results in a nasty hangover. Perhaps you know the pounding headache and regret of financial, sexual, popularity, or career hangover. Again, no judgment here, just honesty. We started out looking for fulfillment or fun but woke up to reality one day with our heads hanging low and a lot of apologies that needed to be made.

God's love and grace unlock everything that you've truly ever wanted: peace, healing, purpose, and the promise of truly lasting transformation.

In Galatians 5:1, we're reminded that as believers that we've been made free in Christ. This is such good news in the wake of whatever you feel is holding you hostage today, whether it seems like you are stuck in a prison of your past, your problems, or your pain. In my *Breakthrough: Finding Freedom in Christ* Bible study, I define freedom in Christ as a life free from fear and fully alive in God's great adventure of joy and purpose for your life. Freedom in Christ isn't a list of rules or performance standards that you've got to measure up to for God's approval. God's love and grace unlock

Why Do We Need to Find Jesus in the Psalms?

everything that you've truly ever wanted: peace, healing, purpose, and the promise of truly lasting transformation.

For those who shirk off God's invitation to freedom in favor of following their own way, God laughs. In fact, that opens the following verse 4: "But the one who rules in heaven laughs. / The LORD scoffs at them" (Psalm 2:4).

Again, how many times has God seen different rulers throughout humanity attempt to eliminate Christianity to silence the influence of God? One of the most notable and brutal attempts occurred in 303 CE when Roman Emperor Diocletian started the Diocletianic or Great Persecution, known as the last, yet most brutal persecution of Christians.

At first, Diocletian was content to let Christians live with their religious freedom, but in time, he changed the laws, demanding that they follow pagan practices. After destroying churches and existing Christian books, he ordered that clergy be arrested unless they recanted.[12] Then, Diocletian's soldiers were ordered to find Christians and force them to recant their allegiance to Christ or face death. As a result, the blood of countless martyrs flowed. Christians were murdered, whether locked and burned in their homes, executed by arrows or swords, or subject to all manner of early torture devices. One city, Phrygia, comprised of mainly Christians, was burned to the ground. Reports included that even Christians within the emperor's own staff were executed because they refused to denounce their faith. Yet, he wasn't the only ruler who attempted to stamp out the flame on the gospel, nor the light of Christ in the world.

For all the horror that Diocletian and other rulers have inflicted on the world to eliminate the influence of Christ, they all have one thing in common: They've failed.

Therefore, God laughs. He scoffs because they foolishly think that their human effort can stop an eternal power.

Yet, God's laughter quickly converts to anger. While heaven shields God's holy contempt, we can have faith that just because we can't always connect the dots between God's anger and earthly outcomes, God isn't letting the wickedness of those who destroy God's people go unpunished. I don't know about you, but I hate feeling powerless to fight against the darkness in our world. I stopped watching television years ago because I was quickly overwhelmed by the sheer amount of pain and heartache in our world and my heart couldn't hold it all without staying in a constantly broken state. Yet, rather than blaze with bitterness or begin to strike back at the surface of a dark and deep spiritual battle, I am reminded of two verses:

> Dear friends, never take revenge. Leave that to the righteous anger of God. For the Scriptures say,
>
> "I will take revenge;
> I will pay them back,"
> says the LORD.
>
> (Romans 12:19)

> For we are not fighting against flesh-and-blood enemies, but against evil rulers and authorities of the unseen world, against mighty powers in this dark world, and against evil spirits in the heavenly places.
>
> (Ephesians 6:12)

Both verses remind me that God is still in control of a world that looks, sounds, and acts like it's gone mad. Even on our best day, we're not equipped to battle the depravity of what's really behind our biggest problems. Yet, we can live with hope that God sees, and even when those mighty, dark powers are directed our way, God hasn't left us defenseless. He's also not surprised, and even as waves of Christians throughout time have called for Jesus's return because we happen to be tired of the world's shenanigans, God seems to be biding his time. He's patient with our hurting world, even though he knows that for some of us that pain runs deep.

As David records God's proclamation to Jesus in Psalm 2:8-9, we see that the earth belongs to the Messiah, which will later be revealed as Jesus, whether the rulers acknowledge it or not.

Why Do We Need to Find Jesus in the Psalms?

Only ask, and I will give you the nations as your inheritance,
the whole earth as your possession.
You will break them with an iron rod
and smash them like clay pots.

(Psalm 2:8-9)

Unfortunately for unbelieving world rulers, their dreams of domination will be smashed into pieces.

In Revelation, we read of a new heaven and a new earth, redeemed from the stain of sin and the tears of our consequences. As believers, we can look forward to that day, but David writes how God prophesies that his anointed one will smash the world's rulers and kings like clay pots. In fact, before going into battle, ancient kings used to smash clay pots to symbolize how they would defeat their enemies.[13]

There's a vast debate and discussion that we could have around the big questions pertaining to the end of the world. Scholars debate the who, what, when, where, why, and how, but at the end of the day, the exact details of the final phase of human history here on earth remain with God alone (Matthew 24:36-38). Our hope rests in the assurance of God's victory, not knowing the details of when or how it will happen.

In the last portion of Psalm 2, David turns his attention back to the rulers of the world, this time warning them with an invitation to turn toward God. He implores them to see Yahweh as sovereign instead of relying on the power of their thrones. Even as they rule, they cannot and will not rule forever.

While most of us will never ascend as rulers or carry worldwide influence, there's still the matter of the little kingdoms that you and I set up in our own hearts where we perch ourselves on little demigod thrones. We long to rule over our own lives and only invite God in when it's convenient. Perhaps, David's writings in Psalm 2 have stirred thoughts about your own life. What if we take a moment to step back and to reflect?

Reflection is a word that describes the mental rewind and reviewing of what's already occurred. It's an intentional process of thinking about our thinking or examining the path of what we're feeling. One of the tools that I created for my own reflection is what I call the Spiritual ABC's: *spiritual attitude, spiritual behavior,* and *spiritual character.* Using the following rubric: Red Light, Yellow Light, or Green Light, how do you see yourself in each of these three areas. *Note: Be kind to yourself.*

- **Spiritual Attitude:** *What is your level of connection with God or willingness to live for eternal priorities?*
- **Spiritual Behavior:** *What do your normal actions or activities indicate is your level of obedience or surrender to God?*
- **Spiritual Character:** *How often do you present yourself to be Spirit-led, or when does your internal or external life look like Jesus?*

The red light, yellow light, green light system is only intended to be an indicator, not a judge or condemnation. Whatever you assign isn't as important as what you discern from God as a space of repentance or even possible next steps. This process is intended to open up opportunities to build authenticity with God, not barriers to hide behind.

As you reflect, specific moments may come up like the time when you said something to your kids or all of the times when you didn't put your cell phone down to look into your spouse's eyes. That stuff happened and you're willing to acknowledge it. But don't get stuck there. As they say, "Look back, but don't stare."

At the end of any reflection, give yourself a smile for you've created space for God.

The final verse of Psalm 2 declares a precious blessing when we make sure that our hearts rest with God in a world that rebels against him: "But what joy for all who take refuge in him!"

CHAPTER TWO

Finding Jesus with Us in Our Hard Places

CHAPTER TWO

Finding Jesus with Us in Our Hard Places

Scripture Reading: Psalm 16

"Now's your opportunity," whispered his men. They'd seen what he'd been through. They'd been on the run with him. They wanted him to do what some of them probably dreamed of doing for themselves.

Kill the king.

David had been on the run from King Saul for a long time. At first, he was alone. Then, his brothers, other relatives, and a group of men described as "in trouble or in debt or who were just discontented" (1 Samuel 22:2), about 400 men total, gathered around David. Initially, the raggedy group of disreputable men were afraid to fight (1 Samuel 23:3). But after God helped them defeat the Philistines, more men joined their ranks. As David's warriors fled once again from a murderous King Saul and Israelite army, the men eventually made their way into a stronghold or place of refuge named En-Gedi.

For a while, David and his men lived without interference at En-Gedi. King Saul stopped chasing David because he had to pivot and return to fight the Philistines. But, like the proverbial bad penny, King Saul resurfaced again, looking to kill David. David drew the king's ire because he had God's favor as warrior and future king of Israel. His successes on the battlefield stirred the sour stew of jealousy, regret, and anger within King Saul's soul. He poured out his wrath on David, forcing his former protégé to leave everything that was familiar and uproot his life in order to stay alive.

Sounds unfair, doesn't it?

Life is frustrating when it's unfair.

Have you had any moments this past year when you whispered under your breath, "Why'd you let that happen, God?" or "It wasn't supposed to be this way!" Based on our human tendencies to focus on the negative, you wouldn't be unusual if your mind tends to stay locked and loaded on whatever is missing, broken, or changed instead of the positive.

If you're in a season of life and feeling like a bit of a hostage, or someone who feels forced to engage this study or guilted into going to church when you're mad at God, you aren't alone. There have been many times at which I've prayed and asked God to right a wrong and it hasn't happened. I've had to learn how to wade through the pools of pain and sidestep the road that could certainly lead to bitterness and keep my eyes on seeking out the En-Gedi spaces of rest and refuge, even if they only existed in my times of prayer or solitude.

Unfairness leaves us with a sense of loss or imbalance. It can mess with our emotional barometer of safety and security. It's a human reality that has always made me exceedingly uncomfortable. I remember the many times that my dad told me that life wouldn't be fair. It wasn't as if I was stomping around the house yelling, "It's not fair!" In fact, there was no yelling or stomping in our home. My parents didn't play that. But I believe that God gave my dad special discernment about his first-born daughter whose stubborn heart rebelled against anything that didn't align with my personal quid pro quo such as:

If someone does something nice for you, then you should do something nice back.
If someone is good, then good things should happen to them.
If one works hard enough, then they should be rewarded.

Do you have any "If…thens" that haven't turned out how you'd thought? How much frustration do those unmet expectations create for you?

In that cave, David's men whispered their battlefield version of quid pro quo: "*If King Saul is trying to kill you, then you have the right to kill him first*" (1 Samuel 24:4).

So much of what makes our lives hard or what frustrates us are the *"If…thens"* expectations that we live by. We see the way that the world should be and when life or people flow different, we can get frustrated, even bitter.

At many points in David's life, he experienced hardship because he obeyed God when it would have been easier to exact a little quid pro quo. One of those times was when King Saul had to do, well, what humans must do:

Saul went into a cave to relieve himself. But as it happened, David and his men were hiding farther back in that very cave!

*"Now's your opportunity!" David's men whispered to him. "Today the L*ORD *is telling you, 'I will certainly put your enemy into your power, to do with as you wish.'"*

(1 Samuel 24:3b-4)

There was David hiding in a cave at the same time when King Saul unknowingly put himself in a vulnerable and possibly fatal posture. Could you imagine what the royal record could have looked like if David had killed Saul in that moment? KING SAUL ASSASSINATED WHILE GOING TO THE BATHROOM. That would have been embarrassing. David's men were all for revenge. Perhaps their nudge was motivated by a desire to vicariously experience an emotional win all the places where they felt like they'd lost in other places in their lives.

However, David doesn't kill Saul. He makes a move that doesn't quite reflect the strategy of a seasoned warrior like himself. He sneaks up and cuts off a piece of the hem of Saul's robe. What's wild is that David exclaimed guilt for even that benign action! Still, he also ordered his men not to kill Saul, which they probably wanted to do since David didn't.

What is it about David that he could stand firm in a situation where he could right a wrong, re-balance the scales, and eliminate an enemy? David put his security in God, not in trying to control his earthly situation.

As you are reflecting on the seasons in life that haven't gone as planned or if you're presently wrestling with lingering unfairness or frustration of missed expectations, Psalm 16 offers us a chance to peek into David's life-giving perspective on why he was so committed to God at times when he might have wondered if God cared. My prayer is that you'll see how God cares for us.

Five Lessons from David's Life in Psalm 16

This week, we're studying Psalm 16, traditionally ascribed to the authorship of King David mainly because of attribution by one of the early church leaders, Peter, in Acts 2. In addition to Peter confirming David's authorship, this is considered a messianic psalm because Peter also preached that Psalm 16 pointed to Christ and the Apostle Paul taught the same in his sermon at Antioch (Acts 13:35). There's a particular section of this Psalm that we'll study this week that points directly to Jesus, but the rest of the Psalm also rings with five gospel-connected themes that can enrich our Lenten reflections this Easter season.

Why does it matter that New Testament leaders confirm David's authorship? While this is a deep and broad topic, taking note of when New Testament leaders confirm Old Testament writings is an internal test of reliability that we can look to as confirmation of biblical consistency. That doesn't necessarily confirm reliability or authenticity, but there are other tests that address those elements. In this case, the fact that the early church leaders confirm and quote Psalm 16 under the authorship of David is something that we can tuck away into cerebral cloud storage systems and say, "Okay, so David did write that."

As far as background goes, there isn't an agreed upon timeline for when this psalm was written. One scholar suggests that it might have been after God confirmed to David that his throne would last forever, which boosts the messianic reference later in the chapter.[1] An interesting note: Psalm 16 is unique in that it is the first psalm labeled as a *miktam* or *michtam*. Even though it's the label or heading of the psalm, there is a question around what a "Miktam of David" actually means. One scholar gives a range of possibilities: "engraved in gold, to cover, a secret treasure, a poem containing pity sayings."[2] Psalms 56–60 are also labeled as *miktams* as well.

For those who love learning unique tidbits about scripture, you're welcome. Now, with the introduction of a mysterious word that isn't understood, sometimes that stokes healthy curiosity, which is a good thing! On the other hand, it might stir confusion, questions, or even skepticism. *Here's yet another thing in the Bible that I don't understand!* Whenever I run across something in scripture that isn't clearly defined, I like to ask myself the question: "At this moment, does this need to be answered in order for me to trust Jesus?" Sometimes, we've got to dig into scripture, especially when we're searching or confused, but there are other times when we can make a note about something we're unsure of and research it later.

In Psalm 16, the first verse gives us insight into why David didn't need to exact revenge on Saul through either killing him or some other way of evening the score: "Keep me safe, O God, / for I have come to you for refuge" *(Psalm 16:1).*

It's not clear whether David was in danger when writing this psalm. There are psalms that document times in David's life when he was on the run or he's in an unsettled emotional place. In this upbeat psalm, David shares where he finds his safety and security in life. Whether David is hiding in a cave or comfortable in his palace in later life, God was the sole source of David's safety and security.

I live in an area of the country where tornados pop up from time to time. While I've never lived through a tornado, perhaps you or someone that you know has endured that terrifying experience. I have been through some close calls. From kindergarten through high school, I remember seasonal tornado drills. The alarm would sound and our teacher would lead us to the designated safe place in our building, often an interior hallway where we'd get down on our knees in front of a row of lockers and wrap our hands over our heads. Even as we were in the safest place we could be, I still remember my little heart beating fast and my little mind wondering whether we'd really be safe if there really was a tornado.

As a parent, I trained my children from an early age to go to the basement and sit under the stairwell if a tornado siren went off and I wasn't home. Now, that my kids are grown up and gone and I live in a different location, my tornado plan is to hop in my bathtub and pull a mattress over my head. No matter the plan, the goal is to get to a place of safety and protection. But, there are no absolute guarantees here on earth.

> **When it comes to finding a place of safety and security for our hearts and minds, we are assured of God's presence and protection.**

Yet, when it comes to finding a place of safety and security for our hearts and minds, we are assured of God's presence and protection. How do we get to that place? How do we get to a place of safety and protection for our hearts and minds when the tornado of a lost job sweeps through or a tornado of a child's rebellion, a devastating diagnosis, or a category-five twister destroys the future that you'd dreamed for yourself? Without a place where we feel emotionally safe and secure, our hearts risk being ripped to shreds and our faith torn apart by the tornados of life.

In Psalm 16, David offers five observations about how finding refuge in God blesses his life in the present as well as his future:

1. **David believed in God's goodness.**

   In Psalm 16:2, David says that "Every good thing I have comes from you." Again, since we don't know exactly when David writes those words, there may be painful situations in his life that haven't happened yet, like his adultery, the sexual assault of his daughter, or the attempted overthrow by his son. Yet, David had already experienced challenging times in his early life, like the many years on the run from Saul. So, when David says that God has given him every good thing, he has tasted and seen that God is good. Maybe he's thinking about all his victories in battle, the times that he fell in love or perhaps the long, solitary days in the wilderness on the run when he worshipped God and felt a close connection with him. In Psalm 103:5, David writes, "He fills my life with good things" as an overall declaration of how God has shown up in his life.

   When I looked up the Hebrew translation for "good" the word is *towb*, also transliterated as *tov*, as in *mazel tov*.[3] This happens to be a favorite word of mine. Not only does *towb* mean "good," but it also means "beautiful." Genesis 1 uses *towb* repeatedly to describe God's reflection on what he'd created, which makes sense because if God's character is good, then everything that he would create would bear his goodness. So, as David reflects on his remarkable life, he can see God's goodness fingerprinted all over his life.

Depending on your perspective, it might be hard for you to embrace that God is good or that he has filled your life with good things. Perhaps as you're reflecting on your whole life or even the past year of your life, you sense a little distance between yourself and God. You've questioned whether God is good. Whether it's the events happening in our world or in your home, the intensity of the bad seems to overwhelm your ability to believe that God is good.

When you don't believe that God is good, then it's going to be a challenge to see God as a safe space, especially if you question whether God is responsible for those bad things. I had a conversation with someone who'd been praying for years that a relationship would be restored and it didn't happen. That circumstance temporarily shook their belief in God's goodness. They needed time to realize that they'd allowed a singular event to become their definition of God's goodness. Once that *aha* moment made itself known, their challenge was to decide whether they would disconnect God's goodness from the outcomes of their prayers or circumstances.

For me, I've had to learn the difference between "God is good" vs. God *is* good. The former is what we often say when we get what we want. It's when we pray and God answers in a way that makes us smile and happy. This is a situation declaration that can change depending on how or when our prayers are answered. However, the latter statement is a character declaration about God, which has nothing to do with our circumstances. As one writer says, "He is void of anything that is not good, and everything that is good has its origins in God."[4] For the record, God *is* good, whether you believe it or not. However, what you believe will impact your experience and your ability to find safety and security within God's promises and presence in your life.

Finding Jesus with Us in Our Hard Places

God isn't good only when we're happy or when our prayers are answered. God *is* good. God is the ultimate in goodness no matter our situation or current state of mind, even if the beginning, middle, or end of our life or situation feels bad. God's goodness means that he has the power to bring beauty from ashes and ugly from awful. The fact that God *is* the definition of goodness is the reason we can have hope, peace, and joy in hard circumstances.

2. **David delighted himself with godly people.**

In verse three, David celebrates the godly people around him. In one translation, he calls them "his heroes." Again, without a firm timeline on when this psalm was written, it's hard to say who was in David's life at that time. We do know that there were a few people who weren't for David at times like King Saul and his wife Micah, who saved his life from Saul once, but later treated David with contempt and made fun of him for dancing before God (2 Samuel 6:16). However, maybe David writes and remembers that raggedy army of men that turned into quite a gathering of faithful warriors, including a set of men known as the Three and the Thirty (2 Samuel 23). At one time, while David was holed up in the cave, he remarked about how he wanted a fresh drink of water from the well at Bethlehem. A group of those men fought through the Philistines to get David a drink, which he promptly poured on the ground as an offering in recognition of the men's bravery. Personally, I would have felt like I needed to drink the water, but David's men saw the honor in his actions.

Then there was Nathan. He was the prophet who spoke God's truth and correction in David's life. Nathan is best known for confronting David after the affair with Bathsheba and after David's orders to set up her husband to be killed in battle. As painful as Nathan's confrontation with David was, it was a pivotal moment that allowed

David to own up to his sin and find forgiveness and freedom from the aching gnaw of disgust and dishonesty that drained David's spirit (Psalm 32:3, Psalm 51).

As you reflect on different aspects of your life, what kinds of believers surround you? Do you delight in the other believers in your life? Much of our lives involves our relationships and many of those relationships can be with other believers.

This is where the topic gets complicated because in recent years, a needed whistle has been blown on significant numbers of pastors and other influential people in the church. Additionally, there's a name for the unholy, ungodly ways that Christians have treated other believers: spiritual abuse. I want to recognize that there's a sad pall over the body of Christ when it comes to our relationship with each other.

One of my favorite slogans, however, is "keep your eyes on your own Hula-Hoop." I adopted this saying from a family addiction support group. This slogan means that I can focus on what is specifically under my control and whatever is outside of my Hula-Hoop isn't under my control.

As it applies to delighting in other believers, I can choose to seek out and surround myself with both men and women who love like Jesus. You can too. This may mean giving ourselves permission to uproot and relocate ourselves into a different faith community. This could mean establishing boundaries to limit Christians who aren't loving. But, at the end of the day, I must own the responsibility for finding a community of believers that I can delight in.

I don't want to overlook those who have been hurt. Like David, we may have a vindictive Saul or an unsupportive Michal in our lives, which is hard. Yet, I hope that you have a group of faithful warriors like David and wise, trusted voices like Nathan. These are the people who will fight with you, fight for you, and challenge you to pursue God's best in the important battles of life. I hope that you have friends like David's men, who went to great lengths to get him a fresh cup of water, who will show up for you in sacrificial ways when it matters most, and that you show up for them in return.

To summarize, look for people who love Jesus and believe that God IS good. If those people aren't around and you're looking for them, in the meantime, *you* be the inspiration and encouragement!

3. **David was content.**

In verses five and six, David expresses the richness of God's blessing in his life. Again, while David would rule as the king of Israel, he doesn't place his security in his wealth. Note what he says here in verse 5: "LORD, you alone are my inheritance, my cup of blessing."

For David, of all of the wealth that he had in the world, God was his blessing. In the previous verse, David observed the pagan nations who spent their time praying and worshipping impotent gods. Part of their worship included making sacrifices of animals and drinking blood in futile attempt to whip up the favor or blessing of the gods. In some cases, human sacrifices were made, such as child sacrifice to gods like Molech, which is why God expressly prohibited child sacrifice (Leviticus 18:21).

In an ancient world where there was much superstition and much less information than we have today, people thought that the gods would help them make the rain fall, heal their sick, or restore fertility. With the stakes of survival in play, it's not a surprise that desperate times would call for desperate measures like drinking the life blood of another creation. Yet, David had seen and tasted of God's goodness, therefore he had no desire to follow in the pagans' paths. God was enough for him.

This is the sweet spot where we say that we want to be, but how many of us wonder if God will really be enough? Can your relationship with God fill the deep places of longing or satisfaction? We'd rather share how much we weigh with others rather than admit that we doubt that God is enough. Even as we know that God is the creator of good things that we're surrounded by, we're challenged because we've fallen more in love with those good things rather than the Giver who provided them for us.

What does David mean when he says that God is his inheritance? This touches on David's awareness of God's promise to establish an eternal royal lineage through David's bloodline. In fact, in a few verses, David will allude to that "holy one."

Consider David's perspective. He was a king with access to all types of resources and earthly treasure, yet David didn't put his faith in his possessions; he knew that his reward was only found in the riches offered through God. Same for us. Jesus taught in Matthew 6:19-20:

Don't store up treasures here on earth, where moths eat them and rust destroys them, and where thieves break in and steal. Store your treasures in heaven, where moths and rust cannot destroy, and thieves do not break in and steal.

What makes you happy? Whatever it is, great! How can you combine what makes you happy with giving it an upgrade to include an eternal outcome?

Let's take coffee. Coffee does not make me happy; it makes me jittery. However, I know that coffee makes a lot of people very happy. If you adore your daily cup of coffee and hate the idea of living without it, that's business between you and God. Yet, what if you could elevate your love of coffee into an eternal opportunity? For example, as you savor your morning cup, keep a notepad close by and write out a gratitude list. If you enjoy an afternoon cup, get intentional and invite someone who needs encouragement or sip your brew while engaged in an iron-sharpens-iron time with another believer. Or, you can use your coffee breaks to pray for five people in your life or memorize scripture.

Giving up a good thing to experience a greater connection with God can be a transformative blessing that will impact your life on a far greater scale than whatever you gave up in a moment's time.

How much richer and more satisfying could your life be if you engaged in just one of those opportunities? Giving up a good thing to experience a greater connection with God can be a transformative blessing that will impact your life on a far greater scale than whatever you gave up in a moment's time. Consider the ways that you'd grow in contentment and peace with the life that you have instead of the constant message in culture to get "more, more, more."

David never found his contentment in his earthly treasures. He knew that the real riches of life were only found in God's presence and nothing else.

4. **David was assured of God's constant presence.**

David fought through times in life when he questioned whether God had left him alone in the pain and problems that he couldn't solve. For example, right before David fled to En-Gedi, he'd hit a low in his life. Here are his words in Psalm 13:1: "O LORD, how long will you forget me? Forever? / How long will you look the other way?"

He'd been on the run from Saul for some time and David felt like God had forgotten him. That must have felt so discouraging, especially since David knew that he'd be the future king of Israel one day. He was probably like "What gives, God?!" When we read God's promises, but our lives move in painful directions, it can cause us to wonder if God's changed his mind on us or given up on us. Maybe you're dealing with a situation that's been around for so long it's starting to feel like a family pet. When we're praying and it doesn't seem like God is answering, we can question whether he is active and working in our lives.

Throughout the psalms, David is honest with God about the ups and downs of his life. It's so helpful that we see David expressing his low moments and asking hard questions. That kind of candor with God combined with David's worshipful heart makes David's faith stronger. He develops a steadfast trust in God that David sums up in Psalm 16:8: "I know the LORD is always with me. / I will not be shaken, for he is right beside me."

As I reflected on David's words, I was reminded of my children when they were toddlers. There were times when their tempest emotions flared because I swooped them up to keep them from running into the street or stopped them from touching something hot. I rescued them from danger, but that didn't stop them from protesting in my arms. They'd squirm and kick in a great effort to get back down and rush right back into danger. Yet, as I held them tightly, they would calm down and even lay their heads on my shoulder and lean against me. At some point, their inner turmoil and outer tempest would quiet and their worn-out little bodies would rest against me.

Isn't that a picture of what David is writing about and what God wants for us? To know that we can settle ourselves against God and allow him to quiet the anxieties and wrestling in our hearts?

I wonder if there was a specific memory that David was thinking about as he made this declaration. Maybe he wasn't thinking about just one moment in time. Perhaps, he'd strung together all the times when he remembered how God was present in the highest moments as well as the problems and painful moments in his life. God's presence is a reality whether we can see it or feel it. As C. S. Lewis says, "We may ignore, but we can nowhere evade the presence of God. The world is crowded with him. He walks everywhere incognito."[5]

Often, it's reflection that equips us to see in reverse what we didn't see at the moment. Think about some of the difficult circumstances in your childhood. If you look back at those circumstances through your adult eyes and with a Jesus-filter, noting the divine moments and unique blessings, you should be able to see God's activity in your circumstance. While there may have been pain, tears, or even devastation, since we live in a broken and fallen world, that doesn't mean that the power and presence of God wasn't there in that moment.

This is what David understood for his life. He knew that the faithful God of his past would remain the steadfast God of his future so that he could face future challenges without the fears that whisper, "What if I can't handle this?" or "Why is God letting this happen to me?" When we stand unshakable in faith and trust, we will still face problems and pain, but we don't question whether God is present in the moment.

5. **David had an eternal perspective.**

Our human history has been filled with world leaders, politicians, and powerful individuals concerned with their power grab in the here-and-now. Even though their antics and tactics turn our stomach, how many of us secretly wish that we had a sliver of their wealth and influence to get what we want?

For an earthly king, David lived with a heavenly outlook, which is quite admirable. As king, David would have been surrounded by the best of the best. Yet, that wasn't his focus.

While David lived in ancient times, many centuries before this moment that we're sharing today, he still had a sense of God's big picture and greater timeline than just his life.

Early in his life, David was called "a man after his [God's] own heart" (1 Samuel 13:14). This characterization was attributed to David in light of the failure of Israel's first king, Saul, to be faithful to God. No one else in the Bible carries such a label about their lives. The closest other label was John, who referred to himself as the disciple that Jesus loved (John 13:23).

Being a man after God's own heart didn't mean that David was perfect. We know that he wasn't. And maybe, this offers us some much-needed hope. Consider this, the scriptural author wrote that David was a man after God's own heart even as David's imperfect up and down life would lead us to question whether that attribution was a mistake. It wasn't! David's life is a reminder to us that it's in our imperfections, our cracks and brokenness, that the light of Christ and God's transforming power shines through us as a powerful testimony to others. If you remember the story of the woman at the well in John 4, the reason why the people in the village came to believe in Christ was because after she proclaimed that Jesus saw her in her complicated story, they came to hear Jesus and their lives were changed. It's a much-used saying, but always powerfully true: *God can use any mess in your life to create a message that blesses you and others!*

It's easy to take ourselves to task for all the places where we should have done something different or better. Can we invite the gift of grace that Jesus died to bring us into our flaws and failures? Like Jesus did with the woman at the well, we can tell ourselves the truth without tearing ourselves down.

We will fall at times and experience the consequences of our sin as well as the impact of others' sin on our lives. Yet, we can follow in David's footprint and have hearts that love God and love the things that God loves. We can trust God, like David. We can always worship God, like David. We can repent to God, like David. We can champion God's ways to the people around us, like David.

Shouldn't we find it inspiring that a man who was an earthly king wrote over half the Psalms in worship to a heavenly God? Think about it, how many world leaders do you know that would undertake such a task? Can you imagine a current president, king, or dictator in our world writing a book of praises to God and publishing it for the world to see and read? Not impossible, but also, not likely.

Once a ruler in our world dies, the world shifts its attention to the next ruler that will take his or her place. No matter how influential or how long a ruler was in charge, their power comes to an end. There's a folklore around ancient conqueror Alexander the Great's final requests that included his body being carried by doctors with precious jewels, like gold, lining their mourning path and Alexander's lifeless hands hanging outside of his coffin.

It appears that Alexander understood the limitations of humanity and the realities of eternity. As he lay dying at only thirty-two years old after conquering large segments of the world, Alexander requested that doctors carry him because he wanted the people to know that there are limitations that not even doctors can overcome. The jewels? Alexander wanted the wealth that he acquired to be spread on the streets as a reminder that not even wealth can stop death. Finally, his request for his hands to be buried outside of his coffin was to be a reminder that no one can take anything from this world.

While these final requests from Alexander the Great are debated as popular lore, they do underscore wisdom that Jesus taught in Matthew 6:19-20 and also, a wisdom that David understood in his lifetime.

In Psalm 16:10, David writes: "for you will not leave my soul among the dead." As David reflected on his life, his goal wasn't to see how much wealth he could accumulate, rather his eyes were already fixed and focused on a life beyond the grave. Other translations identify a specific place for the dead called *Sheol*, translated in Hebrew as an underworld where people descend at death (Genesis 37:35, Isaiah 38:10).[6] While we're used to thinking about the afterlife in the context of heaven and hell because of what we know about grace and the gospel, David lived before Christ, but he had a knowledge beyond himself about the afterlife because David knows that Sheol won't be his final resting place; rather his eternity will be spent in God's presence.

Jesus and Psalm 16

In the latter portion of Psalm 16:10, David speaks of the "holy one" that God would not leave in the grave.

For all the technology that our world has created, we still haven't been able to make headway on stopping death. While science is creating technologies, like cryogenics, that hope to bring the dead back to life in the future, the reality is that death is a certainty of our human experience.

God has created us with an awareness, even a longing, for an eternity after this life is over.

Whether our world wants to acknowledge it or not, God has created us with an awareness, even a longing, for an eternity after this life is over.

Finding Jesus with Us in Our Hard Places

Even in our post-Christian American culture, most people are still comforted by the idea that a loved one is in heaven rather than just cold and lifeless in the ground.

On a layover in Dallas, I settled into a seat to enjoy some chocolate frozen yogurt with chocolate-peanut butter candies on top. Only halfway through my long cross-country flight, I needed a pick-me-up and I wanted to eat it in peace and quiet. As I scooped the last portion of my treat, a gentleman sitting next to me asked how long our flight was delayed. I had to listen carefully and adjust my ears to understand his Mexican-infused English. That brief exchange opened up a conversation. Now, when one is in the airport, there are lots of topics that people can discuss. Usually, it's the weather, our destination, travel nightmare stories, and so forth. However, this man wanted to talk about something different. He wanted to talk about death.

He grabbed one of the two cell phones sitting in front of him to show me the pictures of his nineteen-year-old nephew's recent funeral. Even as I could only understand every few words he spoke, each picture lived up to their proverbial thousand words of communication, speaking volumes to me about life, sadness, family, and grief. The man showed me photos and videos of his young, strong nephew riding a horse in Mexico, helping with a construction project on their family property, and carrying the coffin of his grandfather as a pallbearer, only two months before his untimely death. Then, the man showed me photos of the young man's funeral. Frankly, it was uncomfortable to see the photos of such an intimate family heartache. Yet, each of his phones, one for when he's in America and the other for when he's in Mexico, carried dozens of photos of family members wearing a graphic t-shirt with the young nephew's photo on the front. There were many pictures of them in front of the coffin, even photos including infants, who the family wanted to be in the photos as well.

As he showed me the photos, the one that seemed most precious was a screen shot of a certificate from their church. Even though I've traveled to central America almost a dozen times, my grasp on the language hovers just above pathetic. I couldn't understand all the words on the certificate, but I could make out just enough to know that the document affirmed the young man's destination in heaven upon his death. That brought tremendous hope to the man as I pointed to it in the photo. It was one of the few times that he smiled during our conversation.

I didn't have a conversation about Jesus or the gospel with the man that day. Instead, I was reminded that in the face of death, our human souls long to know that there is something beyond the grave. Is this true for you? In the hardest, heartbreaking moments in life, believers can hold onto hope when we know that life isn't bound only by the existence of our heartbeat on earth; rather we've always got an eternity with Christ to look forward to in heaven.

David knew about the Messiah, but not the Jesus that we've come to know. Through the prophet Nathan, David knew that God would raise up one of David's offspring and secure his royal throne forever (2 Samuel 7:16), but David didn't know the details. It's in this hope that David declares that God would not leave his "holy one" in the grave.

David's words point to a messianic message that Jesus himself affirms in John 10:28-29:

> *I give them eternal life, and they will never perish. No one can snatch them away from me, for my Father has given them to me, and he is more powerful than anyone else. No one can snatch them from the Father's hand.*

For Jesus to give eternal life, he must be eternal. Not only that, but Jesus reminds us that we can have security in our eternity. Depending on your religious tradition or the voices around you, there might be a sense that you've got to earn God's favor and even if you do, you're still at risk of losing it if you mess up big enough. Perhaps right now, you question whether God can still love you or if you've done something—anything—that could cancel your salvation. Gratefully, Jesus's words in John 10:28-29 provide the security in your eternity that you need. Read that passage above again and allow Jesus's words to seal up any remaining doubts in your heart or mind. Jesus provides the full and final answer. Will Davis, Jr., writes,

> As long as a believer is worrying about whether they are truly saved, they will never grow up in spiritual maturity. It basically guarantees that a Christian will remain stuck in spiritual infancy. And worse, it paints a picture of God that is not only untrue but also unbiblical. It cheapens the gift of salvation—the gift of grace—and makes God look like a finicky human.[7]

David knew that God could be trusted, and we can trust God as well.

In fact, as Peter teaches to the thousands who'd gathered on the Day of Pentecost after Jesus ascended into heaven, he repeats an entire section of Psalm 16 and David's looking into the future and speaking of the Messiah's resurrection. God would not allow the Messiah, later to be revealed as Jesus's body, to rot in the grave. Just as death wasn't the end for Jesus, it isn't the end for us.

As David ends the Psalm, his words seem to be a fitting end for this chapter. May his words bring hope, joy, and peace into your life as you navigate the hard spaces, knowing that God is by your side:

You will show me the way of life,
    granting me the joy of your presence
    and the pleasures of living with you forever.
                    (Psalm 16:11)

SPIRITUAL JOURNEY REFLECTION

Using the following rubric: Red Light, Yellow Light, or Green Light, how do you see yourself in each of these three areas in the past week. *Remember: Be kind to yourself.*

- **Spiritual Attitude:** *What is your level of connection with God or willingness to live for eternal priorities?*
- **Spiritual Behavior:** *What do your normal actions or activities indicate about your level of obedience or surrender to God?*
- **Spiritual Character:** *How often do you present yourself to be Spirit-led, or when does your internal or external life look like Jesus?*

CHAPTER THREE

Finding Jesus as Our Shepherd

CHAPTER THREE

Finding Jesus as Our Shepherd

> *Scripture Reading:*
> *Psalm 23; John 10:1-18*

On his way home from school, a young Russian boy noticed a lamb trapped head down in a drainage ditch. He went home and asked his mother to come back and help him get the stranded animal free. Azieva Radima went back to the trench with her son. As he worked to free the lamb, she pulled out her camera to capture the ordeal. She planned to record a message encouraging others not to leave animals in trouble. In a video that went viral around the world, Radima's son looped a strap around its hind leg and began to pull. It was a pretty good size lamb and the young man put a lot of effort into pulling it out of the narrow opening. But he succeeded! The freed lamb hopped away.

But three hops later, it dove headfirst right back into the ditch.[1]

Millions of people around the world have laughed at Radima's video about the lamb that was freed and immediately trapped itself again. As people have posted all types of laughing emojis and comments, the symbolic nature of the sheep's struggle isn't lost on the viewers. Thousands have shared funny, but poignant insights as they relate to the animal's struggle.

> "Getting back together with your ex is like."
> "This is what God does for us."
> "Oh, yeah. I feel that sheep. That seems like the story of my life."
> "When your friends try to help you move on, but…"
> "Not everyone is ready to be rescued…"
> "Hate that I can relate."

I can think of plenty of times in my life when I was trapped in an unhealthy pattern of behavior, disobedience, or difficult situation. I'd pray for God to free me, only to find myself right back in that situation weeks, months, or years later. On the lighter side of a repeated struggle, how many times have I told myself that I will stop waiting to get gas until first thing in the morning, especially when I've got somewhere important to go? Every time, I'm stressed out at the gas pump, running late and praying that I don't spill gas on myself. Of course, I also berate myself and promise to never do it again…until it happens again. On a darker side, there were years when I knew that I needed to let go of control of a situation, but I kept pushing to get my own way, only to hurt others and not move the needle one bit toward the outcome that I was fighting for.

How about you? What are the spiritual struggles in life that you find yourself wrestling with repeatedly? In a recent season, I found myself learning new lessons on patience and trusting God during a time of seemingly unanswered prayer. A little self-righteous anger rose up in me because I'd already spent years learning to be patient in another situation and I was upset that life had me down a new path where new and different lessons had to be learned. I've also spent over a decade learning how to surrender my tendency not to let go of control. It's been a place of precious victory for me. But it's also the place where I will beat myself up whenever I recognize that I've succumbing once more to control-loving behavior.

After watching that viral lamb video a few times, I wondered if the lamb really knew how to avoid getting trapped again? Another thought that I pondered was whether the lamb was so happy to be free that it didn't pay attention to where it was going and that's how it fell in the ditch again.

These musings popped into my mind because like many of the people in the comments, I could also see myself in that lamb. I could see myself in the times when I prayed for God to help me and he did, but over time, I slowly slid back into old habits or an unhealthy behavior. Other times in life, I felt so close to God that I got prideful in everything that I was doing to live out my faith and ended up in shocking places far from God and crying out for help.

In John 8:36, we're reminded that if we've been set free in Christ, we don't have to fear that our salvation will be ripped away if we fall into one of life's inevitable ditches. As believers, we've been set free by receiving what Jesus Christ did for us on the cross. What keeps us stuck in the ditch after making a mistake or experiencing a lapse in faith is believing that we must save ourselves instead of trusting God for our restoration and transformation.

In one of the most well-known passages of scripture, Psalm 23 paints a powerful picture of God's care for our earthly spiritual needs as well as offers rich symbolism that reminds us how God provides for our eternal needs. While you've likely read Psalm 23 on your own, heard it at a funeral, or hung Psalm 23 related artwork on your wall at home, don't skim too quickly over what we're about to share together. God's Word meets us in unique ways each time that we encounter it. So, this means that no matter how many times in your life that you've read Psalm 23, there's an opportunity for a fresh insight each time. That's exciting!

We're going to examine the ways that Jesus's life and message unfold in this psalm. It's a rich and powerful message for us! Additionally, we'll weave John 10, Jesus's teaching on himself as the Good Shepherd, through our exploration of Psalm 23 so that we can draw life-giving insights and connections to how

David's description of God as our Shepherd translates to our understanding of Jesus as Our Good Shepherd for our life today.

Jesus as Good Shepherd

In John 10, Jesus teaches about the Good Shepherd just after the story of his healing a man blind from birth and the resulting religious circus (John 9). The religious leaders questioned the man and his parents before attacking Jesus, who alleged that the Pharisees were spiritually blind because they couldn't see the Savior right in front of them, but the newly seeing man could.

At the beginning of John 10, Jesus begins talking about anyone who tries to get into a sheepfold must be a thief or a robber, meaning that they aren't there for the benefit of the sheep. This is a sharp and critical characterization of the religious leaders. More on that in a moment.

Then, Jesus transitions back to defining the characteristics of a good shepherd:

- Sheep recognize his voice and come to him.
- He knows each by name.
- He goes before them.
- He is the gatekeeper so no danger gets in nor can the sheep get out.
- He sacrifices himself for his sheep.

As Jesus talks about the qualities of the good shepherd, he also highlights how bad shepherds don't protect their sheep and don't care about what happens to them. This reflects the prophet Ezekiel's warning to the religious leaders. Here's one verse of many that outlines their terrible behavior toward the people of Israel even though the priests and the leaders were ordained to care for God's people:

You have not taken care of the weak. You have not tended the sick or bound up the injured. You have not gone looking for those who

Finding Jesus as Our Shepherd

have wandered away and are lost. Instead, you have ruled them with harshness and cruelty.

(Ezekiel 34:4)

Those bad shepherds did exactly the opposite of what Jesus described above, and apparently their ways hadn't changed much from the time of the Old Testament prophet. The prophet Ezekiel makes mention of David later in this chapter. After describing the disgraceful behavior of the bad shepherds, God prophesies through Ezekiel saying that he will gather his sheep back together and take care of them. While this alludes to the point in history when the Jewish people were in captivity in Babylon, there is a point at which David's name is mentioned as God talks about gathering his people under one shepherd. This is a prophetic message about Christ, even though David's name is used. "He is called David, because he sprung from David according to the flesh."[2]

It's a shame to acknowledge that bad religious shepherds have been around for a long time. As one who grew up in the church and spent a large portion of my adult life on staff at a church or working as a full-time Christian author, my heart hurts for those who've been wounded by bad shepherds. It's painful hearing the stories and seeing the revelations of bad behavior by those who are supposed to lead God's people. If this is your story, I am so sorry.

I have my own bumps and bruises from moving within the walls of the church. For me, I find comfort in knowing that beyond what I see in humanity, Jesus is the Good Shepherd who has never let us down.

If there was a singular "why" behind Jesus calling himself the "The Good Shepherd" it's because he's setting the stage for how he will eventually sacrifice his life for his sheep and how he is willing to submit himself to God's great plan for humanity (John 10:18).

In the next section, you'll read David's observation of God as his Shepherd. Unlike David, we have the advantage of seeing how David was writing about Jesus in this psalm. As you read through

David's observations, see them in the context of Jesus as the Good Shepherd who provides, protects, empowers, and is present in every area of your life.

Why Would David Write Psalm 23?

Psalm 23 was written around 1000 BCE, and David was likely king. Why would David write about being a shepherd at this point in his life? Maybe it's like Hollywood celebrities who write their memoirs about their humble beginnings in life. While their stories are centered around childhood memories, David draws upon youthful experiences as a shepherd and it's not a surprise that his observations not only create meaningful observations for us, but also cast a vision for just how much Jesus loves and cares for each of us.

Picture young David in your mind's eye. He's got his staff and he's walking along the country watching over his father's sheep. Perhaps you see him eyeballing one sheep that seems to be farther out than the others or another sheep making a loud noise because its foot is stuck in a crevice between rocks. While he's in the field, the prophet Samuel shows up at David's home to talk with David's father, Jesse. God sent Samuel to Jesse because Israel's current King Saul was no longer the man for the job. After inspecting seven of Jesse's sons and hearing God take a pass on all of them, including the few who Samuel thought were sure picks, Samuel asks Jesse if there are any more sons to consider. As you read Jesse's response, make note of where his final son is at: "There is still the youngest," Jesse replied. "But he's out in the fields watching the sheep and goats" (1 Samuel 16:11b).

Young David is summoned back to the house. That young man had no idea that the experience he'd gathered in the fields was about to shape the rest of his life in an unbelievable way. While his brothers may have teased later that David was the "Least Likely to Be Chosen as King," he was tapped to be the next king of God's people and also, a strong symbolic figure in the life of Christ.

Throughout the Bible, there are moments of symbolism that illustrate what's been called the "upside-down" kingdom of God. God just doesn't do things the way that we do. David's selection as Israel's king is an example. He didn't have a reputation, royal bloodlines, family wealth, or military experience, all factors that we associate with a ruler of a country or kingdom.

However, David had God. That was all that he needed to level up.

As Samuel looked at David, he received a message from God. David also received something from God:

And the LORD said, "This is the one; anoint him."...

And the Spirit of the LORD came powerfully upon David from that day on.

(1 Samuel 16:12b-13)

Yet, centuries later, the prophet Isaiah would describe the coming Messiah. Like David, the future king wouldn't have wealth or military experience. He would come from a royal bloodline as one of David's descendants. Again, not the expected presentation of a future king.

I wonder if King David recognized the value of how having been a lowly shepherd influenced how he saw and led others from his palace throne? Various commentators have remarked about how kings in ancient times did see themselves as shepherds for their people.[3] If only that mindset could have continued in our modern times, right? I wonder how often David remembered his younger years roaming the fields counting the sheep, looking for the ones who'd wandered off or seeing in his mind's eye the sheep trotting toward him as he called out their names. As I reflected on these questions, my mind filled with various moments from Jesus's teachings where he used sheep and shepherds as symbols of our spiritual condition and his care for us.

One of the tensions for me with Psalm 23 and well, let me be honest, any other place in scripture is being compared to sheep. I do not look like a sheep. I'm hoping that I've gotten myself together enough that I don't smell or look like sheep (okay, there was that unfortunate stretch in the late '80s where my highly puffed, teased hair could have given a fluffy animal a run for their four-legged money). Let's face it, sheep don't have a great reputation in the intelligence department. I happen to think highly of my intelligence. And yet, from God's perspective I am like a sheep. So are you.

Did you know that sheep are mentioned more times in the Bible than any other animal? There are more than 750 mentions of sheep.[4] Generally, sheep were useful to humans both inside and out. Not only are sheep dietary staples for both meat and dairy, but their wool and sheepskin provide warm clothing.

However, sheep don't have a great track record for self-preservation. While they traveled in herds, individual sheep regularly wandered off and got stuck in serious situations because they just weren't paying attention or didn't notice that their friends had moved on while they were head down and still chomping on the grassy nub. Sheep need a shepherd to lead them to food and water because apparently, unlike other animals, they don't have a solid sense for staying alive or out of trouble on their own. Depending on who you are, this might be feeling very real to you right now.

As I consider the helpless nature of sheep, I am uncomfortably aware that in fact, I can be a lot like sheep. That realization is an affront to my pride, but nonetheless true for me. How many times have I known about God's constant care and love for me, but I still wandered off and got myself stuck in a serious situation? How often have I focused on what I wanted to achieve and let attending church or spiritual friendships lapse and then felt lonely? Without beating yourself up, consider how you relate to sheep for a few moments.

To fully absorb the grace and goodness that God offers through Christ, our part is to humbly see ourselves as the sheep that must be cared for. It doesn't matter if you've got a college degree, corner office, well-paying job, title of pastor or lay leader, or anything else in your life that makes you feel like you're large and in charge. For today, you are a sheep and God has a message for how he wants to care for you in the inside and out, whether you realize that you need it or not.

> *To fully absorb the grace and goodness*
> *that God offers through Christ,*
> *our part is to humbly see ourselves*
> *as the sheep that must be cared for.*

So, in this section, we'll break Psalm 23 down into what I call "The 5 P's" that characterize the Good Shepherd and how these characteristics point to Christ.

PROVIDER

> The LORD is my shepherd;
> I have all that I need.
> (Psalm 23:1)

As the king of Israel, David was subject to no one in his kingdom. He was surrounded with great wealth and he made the rules. Yet David was wise enough to recognize that for everything that he possessed and controlled, David did not have ultimate control. So, right in the first verse of Psalm 23, David acknowledges that God is the sole provider of everything in David's life. This verse is a declaration of confidence. I wonder if David remembered with fondness his responsibility for taking care of his father's sheep.

Perhaps you've seen portraits of Jesus holding a lamb in his arms with a gentle smile on his face. While sheep may not possess the same kind of thinking prowess as humans, they do know how to trust that their shepherd will feed them and make sure they receive water. Do you think that sheep sit up at night anxious about where their next meal will come from or whether they'll have enough water? Sheep aren't stressing and striving over whether they've got to hustle for their daily existence. They simply trust and follow their shepherd to what's been provided for them.

That sounds a little too easy for us as humans, doesn't it? Yet, imagine what your life would look like if you woke up with knowing that God will provide what you need. To be clear, there is a difference between being *expectant* and having *expectations*. When we're expectant, we are confident that something will happen, but we're not fixed on what the specifics of the outcome will look like. Conversely, expectations look like the picture in our mind of how something should play out, and usually, the outcome should be minimally inconvenient or uncomfortable.

Do you think that sheep have expectations about what kind of water or grazing they'd experience each day? *No, no, Mr. Shepherd. We were kinda hoping for a water source that was just a few degrees cooler than this. Can you make that happen instead?* Instead, the sheep were expectant. They only knew to rely upon their shepherd. They weren't fearful about whether there would be provision; they followed their provider. Maybe we could learn a little from the sheep here about confidently trusting our Good Shepherd.

Can you call to memory times when you panicked or spent a sleepless night stressed out over a situation?

Or, can you remember a time after you'd stressed yourself out and God came through with a solution and you felt (forgive me for this) *sheepish*?

If you can dig into your courage for a few moments, be honest with yourself about the expectations that you have around those circumstances. Take a moment and reflect what it would look like for you to be expectant and know that God will provide instead clinging to your expectations.

I remember lying in the bed one night several decades ago praying. It was the week before Memorial Day. Our family had been impacted by recession-related unemployment, and my part-time church administrative staff job was barely enough to cover our kids' tuition at their Christian private school. We lived paycheck to paycheck, and even then, we only made it to the next paycheck by the skin of our teeth. There was no margin at all.

We didn't have plans for Memorial Day because we didn't have money to make plans. Our families lived out of town, and we didn't want our friends to know that we were barely making it. As I lay in the bed with a few tears rolling down the side of my face onto the pillow, I asked God if he could somehow make a way for me to do something special for my family for Memorial Day. I listed off a few things that I'd hoped to do but I'll never forget ending the prayer with, "God, I don't care what an answer to prayer could look like. Anything that you want to do is fine with me." Looking back on those requests now, they were so humble, but for a tired mother of three children, I just wanted a chance to do something, anything. But I needed God's help.

The next morning, I woke up and went to work. At the time, our staff mailboxes were in an open area and everyone had their own mail cubby. I worked for a large church, so at the time, there were forty or so cubbies. I noticed a lone small white envelope in my cubby with my first name printed simply on the front. I flipped it over and slipped my finger under the seal and opened it up. A single crisp $100 bill was in the envelope. That's it. I flipped the envelope back over and to see if I could recognize the handwriting. I searched my cubby to see if I'd missed a note. Nothing. As you can imagine my eyes were wide open as I looked around. No one knew what I'd prayed to God the night before and it wasn't like single $100 bills showed up in my mailbox every week.

We all know that life has some wild up and down swings. It's hard and heartbreaking. Yet, there are moments when God sends tangible reminders that he is working and active in our lives. It doesn't always look like money or an instant fix for whatever is in crisis. Remaining expectant looks like a confident mindset that God will provide an expression of himself whether it's sending someone with a word of godly encouragement, a Holy

Spirit whisper of hope or comfort, a bit of wisdom to illuminate a problem, that way that God extends time to accomplish what couldn't possibility be accomplished in our own capabilities.

OUR PEACE

> *He lets me rest in green meadows;*
> *he leads me beside peaceful streams.*
> (Psalm 23:2)

Would you say that your life was restful or chaotic? If it's too difficult to make a sweeping generalization on what's happening in your life, perhaps it might be helpful to pinpoint specific areas of your life: home, work, friendships. Are they restful or chaotic?

You aren't alone if you feel like the two-year-old toddler scream of the Now-Now-Now in your life drowns out the quiet, introverted You-Should-Really-Be-On-This voice of the important in your life. Whether it's an unreasonable boss who changes their mind every five minutes or a weakened immune system that can trash anything that you've had planned instantly, chaos looks like being hungry, but you're stuck carrying a hot bowl of soup across a cruise ship in choppy water. You're longing for a chance to stop and eat, but it's a constant fight against instability that you aren't sure that you can win. It's exhausting, draining and frankly, discouraging. ,

While we may know people who thrive off chaos or like the attention that comes with crisis, most of us don't. Problem is that we live in a chaotic world and we keep expecting our world to calm down so that we can. That's not how that works.

Chaos is nothing new under the sun. It's not as if the scriptures haven't given us a heads up on this. And this is also why we need to see Jesus in the psalms because we need to be reminded that while there are a suite of "C" words to describe our world—calamitous, critical, callous, and my personal preference, cringe-worthy—the real question is whether or not I'm attuned to the chaos that I'm carrying around within me.

In John 14:27, Jesus said that he came to give us the gift of peace in our hearts and minds. Jesus never said that he came to bring peace to our world. Let's face it, our world doesn't want peace. Our world wants to grab power and live out of the empty destructiveness of pride. Jesus wanted to offer us the gift of peace of heart and mind so that we have a choice of how we want to live our lives. For me, this means that if I'm experiencing chaos or unsettledness, the first question that I tend to ask myself is, "Is there anything within me contributing to the chaos around me, and am I willing to choose Jesus's gift of peace of heart and mind?"

There are times when our circumstances are unpredictable, uncontrollable, or uncomfortable and it has nothing to do with what we've done or said. Perhaps you remember growing up in a home where crisis-driven chaos was normal, and now, a lack of chaos or crisis is still unfamiliar. But, in the same breath, there are spaces where we push into the chaos with our attempts to control, our expectations, or our insecurities. In that case, Psalm 23:2 offers a gift to you today, especially if you are tired of getting roped into the drama of what's happening in you or around you.

There are unique seasons of life that tend to slow down and give us a chance to press pause or reflect, like Christmas, Easter, summer vacations, or even career transitions. If you're in one of those seasons, resist the pull to go-go-go and instead, create a space where you can observe what God is doing around you. It could look like digging into a resource like this, writing in a gratitude journal, or even looking out the window and seeing God's nature in motion. Invite God into that space instead of more motion or activity.

One of my *aha* moments when reading Psalm 23:2 occurred when I considered what God was doing versus what the sheep is doing.

There are two verb phrases that describe what God is doing: *lets me rest* and *leads me*. Notice how that means that David has to allow or submit to what God is doing. Now, pay attention to the destination points: *green meadows* and *peaceful streams*. I'm not a sheep, but I am totally for green meadows and peaceful streams (if I've got a ride back home).

There's a word that we use a lot to describe our path of our human experience: journey. We all take various journeys in life. You may have taken a healthcare journey, a career journey, a parenting journey, or a forgiveness journey. However, the one thing that we can't ignore is that we rarely have control over our progress, the starts and stops along the way, or the outcome.

My *aha* moment was realizing that when I allow God to lead my life journey, the endpoints for me are *green meadows* and *peaceful streams*. Green meadows symbolize abundance. The sheep have all of their needs supplied in the green meadows; God is our supply. Peaceful streams mean living water, just as Jesus taught the woman at the well in John 4. Peaceful streams are where we are replenished when life does wear us down. They represent the fountain of God's strength and refilling of our soul with the peace that's so hard to find in our world today.

So much of our lives are spent trying to grab a lesser version of God's green meadows and peaceful streams. For example, rest. How many of us long for more rest? We've settled for the idea that rest is spending a few hours scrolling on social media or binge-watching anything. Other fake forms of rest include thinking that rest is not going to work, but filling those hours with countless errands or allowing your mind to spin with endless thoughts without quieting your mind.

In his well-known classic, *A Shepherd Looks at Psalm 23*, pastor Phillip Keller recounts his eight years as a sheep rancher in East Africa and other areas in the world. He writes about how sheep don't willingly lie down unless four conditions are met. Here is a summary of what Keller observed:

1. They must be free of fear.
2. They can't feel discord with the other sheep.

3. They have to be free from pesky flies or parasites on their bodies.
4. They can't be hungry.[5]

Look at that list. If you're struggling to tap the brakes on your life and you're convinced that you can never be still, which one of these tends to keep you from fully relaxing without bouncing up to distract yourself or try to sooth yourself?

The first two are self-explanatory, but what about pesky flies or parasites? As I consider our human equivalent, flies are like the constant thoughts buzzing around in our minds and parasites are like anything inside of us draining the life from us, whether it's bitterness, unforgiveness, anger, shame, or any denial of sin. It's hard to be at rest whenever any of those are active within us. Then what about hunger? This is about unmet needs or desires. If we're wrestling with emotional, relational, financial, or spiritual hunger, we'll resist rest.

As our Good Shepherd, God knows what we need. But, he also knows what we need to happen within us before we're willing to allow him to give us what we need. Therefore David's declaration in Psalm 23:1 is important. Remember how he said that not only is the LORD his shepherd, but David also sees that God is the source of all that he needs. David could allow God to lead him to a place of replenishment.

Wrapped in the promises of God are also the reassurances that you and I need to relax into the destination that God longs to lead us. While God makes his promises, ultimately, we must do our part. Our portion isn't finding our own restful places, but trusting that God is our protector, letting go of whatever keeps us from peace with others, allowing God's Holy Spirit to transform our overthinking and to free us from the internal parasites, and surrendering our desire to him. When we do that, we find the sweetness of enjoying what God wants us to receive, both the abundance of his provision and the replenishment of the living water that comes from drawing up the gift given to us through Jesus Christ.

Before we move into the next layer of this verse, contemplate for a moment what David is saying: *When he allows God to oversee his life, God leads him to rest and replenishment.*

POWER

> *He renews my strength.*
> *He guides me along right paths,*
>   *bringing honor to his name.*
>   *(Psalm 23:3)*

When I was nine years old, my parents gave me a handheld PAC-MAN video game. It was the only thing that I wanted for Christmas that year, and I loved that game so much, I kept it until after I got out of college, even though I stopped playing it many years before. As much as I adored having an arcade at my personal disposal, I didn't like the fact that the game required four AA batteries back then. As a nine-year-old, I wasn't exactly flush with cash, so when I realized that the batteries were running low, I begged my mom for replacement batteries. This was in the ancient times before rechargeable batteries or even USB ports. My mom didn't have a "PAC-MAN Game battery" fund just waiting to buy batteries whenever I needed them. Sure, I could request new batteries whenever I wanted, but that didn't mean that my request was at the top of Mom's must-do list. This meant that no matter how badly I wished to play my beloved game, it didn't have the power to do as I wanted.

Our human strength is a lot like those AA batteries. Sure, we may have fully charged batteries at times, but inevitably, the business of life will drain us. For some of you, drained is a regular part of life. Getting through the day is an actual drag. We can attempt to recharge ourselves, but we'll get drained again.

David writes about how the Good Shepherd renews his strength; other translations say "restore." After a lifetime of experiences, David knew the drain of life and circumstances. He knew the pain and heartache of his own mistakes. Instead of seeking wholeness and healing from human effort, David knew that the natural by-product of allowing the Good Shepherd to lead him to restful meadows and replenishing streams would regenerate what life took. Not only that, but after renewal and restoration, David remarks that the Good Shepherd leads him along the righteous paths rather than send David back out to do life on his own.

Many people, including Christians, think that God and fun are as far as the east is from the west. For the record, I was one of those people. While there's a valuable discussion about legalistic religious rules that add unneeded to-do's and do-more's to the gospel, there is also a valuable question to ask around why there are certain things that God asks us to steer clear from.

In Galatians 5, the apostle Paul teaches that when we're living by the Holy Spirit in our lives, that allows us to avoid not only self-generated actions that stack up to derail our lives, but also mindsets that derail our lives (Galatians 5:19-21). How many of us would say that our lives flourished whenever we followed the path of jealousy, fighting with others, or addiction?

God leads us from his love. Anytime that God asks us to do something, it's because he can see down the road of the journey that we can't and he wants to protect us, not penalize us or rob us of pleasure.

In her Bible study, *Finding I AM*, Lysa TerKeurst uses the phrase "protective command" to describe one of the ways that God leads us along righteous paths.[6] God leads us from his love. Anytime that God asks us to do something, it's because he can see down the road of the journey that we can't and he wants to protect us, not penalize us or rob us of pleasure. God knows that, just like the sheep that you read about at the beginning of the chapter that got free and within three hops was back in the ditch, we'll hop into one hot mess after another if we are unwilling to let him lead.

In Isaiah 41:10, the prophet observes that for those who wait on God, letting him lead, their strength is renewed. So, the inverse must be true as well in that we'll end up draining ourselves or crashing into a ditch whenever we get a notion to blaze our own trail in life. Ask yourself this question: Is there an area of your life where it's been hard for you to follow God's leading? Is doing that path alone energizing or draining to your soul?

PROTECTION

> Even when I walk
>   through the darkest valley,
> I will not be afraid,
>   for you are close beside me.
> Your rod and your staff
>   protect and comfort me.
>   (Psalm 23:4)

Shadows find their origins in what is real, but they use darkness to enlarge a shape and distort its reality. We all walk through the "dark valley" in life anytime when we're on the edge of losing what we love or something important to us faces destruction. It's that in-between space where we must acknowledge our reality and then decide how we will live while awaiting to see the outcome. This is one of life's hardest places to be. When I was a kid, I memorized the King James Version of Psalm 23:4, which describes this unsettling place as the "valley of the shadow of death." No matter how we describe it, we all end up there at some point. And our sojourn through that season will absolutely wreck us if we aren't clear that we trust in God or his goodness.

When I was a freshman in college, I received a distress call from home. I rushed hours back home because my eleven-year-old brother was life-flighted to a metro hospital. His skin began splitting apart at the joints and he had a dangerous fever. The doctors diagnosed him with bacterial meningitis. This was decades before a vaccine was available, and right from the beginning, the doctors told us that the odds were against my brother's survival.

A few days later, the doctors gave my parents the grim news. They told us one evening that my brother would pass away by morning. I drove my mother home while my dad stayed at the hospital. As my mother and I sat with our large family Bible, Mom repeated Psalm 23:4 aloud. She was my first Bible teacher and still teaches Sunday school to this day. On that awful night, Mom said, "This was our valley of the shadow of death." She went on to say that as painful and as hard as it was for us to be in that space, God was with us. By a miracle, my brother survived. He spent almost two months in the hospital and almost a year recovering, but he made it.

David evokes the imagery of the Good Shepherd's staying close by his sheep through that valley with his presence and guiding them with his staff, a tool that is an extension of his hands to pull them back from danger, nudge them in the right direction, or fight a predator trying to get to them.

Most importantly, David doesn't fear evil. He is fully aware of evil, but he doesn't fear it and we don't have to either. Evil is a shadow that tries to scare us into believing that It's bigger than God. Evil wants us to believe It can fully destroy us and we'll never come back from Its deeds. Yet, the Good Shepherd in Jesus came and conquered death so that even when we experience an outcome that changes our lives, if someone that we love goes away or dies, or something that we care about ends, evil doesn't have the final say because we know that God redeems and restores whatever evil destroys (Joel 2:25). There is no danger that you will ever face in the dark valley that God's power isn't great enough to save you or sustain you through it.

The challenge is to recognize when you're facing the darkness but never forget that Jesus's light always "shines in the darkness and the darkness can never extinguish it" (John 1:5).

PRESENCE

> *Surely your goodness and unfailing love will pursue me*
> *all the days of my life,*
> *and I will live in the house of the LORD*
> *forever.*
>
> (Psalm 23:6)

This is a sweet way for David to end this illustration of God as the shepherd. Without knowing for sure, perhaps David drew upon Nathan's prophecy of a coming King from David's bloodline who would rule forever, or it could be David's tremendous confidence that his relationship with God would extend beyond the grave. These are incredible words from a man who lived in a palace. While most people would want to hold onto their earthly home forever, David looked forward to his heavenly home, but not the place, rather the eternal position before God's presence.

You may not agree with me, but Christianity has done an awful job conveying the realities of heaven to the rest of the world. Who was it that came up with the chunky, baby-looking angels holding harps and sitting on fluffy clouds? Other associations aren't doing any favors drawing up people in nondescript white robes looking somewhat aimless as they drifted around heaven for an eternal forever.

As David has described the Good Shepherd in Psalm 23 as well as the rest of the psalms, could he be thinking about doing some of the things in heaven that he did on earth, like dancing before the Lord, expressing himself in writing, or even waiting for a chance to build something for God because he wasn't chosen to build the temple on earth? I'm not sure, but what I believe that David knew is that being in the eternal presence of God will be filled with life-giving moments drawn from God because that was David's experience on earth.

I choose to believe that the same will go for us. We may not know everything about heaven, but the same God that created me and you with gifts, talents, desires, and dreams won't strip those aspects of us away once we're in his presence. If anything, we'll have the chance to experience all of that to an unknown greater degree and perfection in his presence. Could it be that earth is our chance to taste eternal life with God before we get to heaven?

My hope is that you've had a chance to experience Psalm 23 in a fresh new way. Seeing Jesus as our Good Shepherd through the eyes of King David as he reflects on his own shepherding years really does offer valuable perspective for our lives today.

SPIRITUAL JOURNEY REFLECTION

Using the following rubric: Red Light, Yellow Light, or Green Light, how do you see yourself in each of these three areas in the past week. *Remember: Be kind to yourself.*

- **Spiritual Attitude:** *What is your level of connection with God or willingness to live for eternal priorities?*
- **Spiritual Behavior:** *What do your normal actions or activities indicate about your level of obedience or surrender to God?*
- **Spiritual Character:** *How often do you present yourself to be Spirit-led, or when does your internal or external life look like Jesus?*

CHAPTER FOUR

Finding Jesus as Our Hope

CHAPTER FOUR
Finding Jesus as Our Hope

> *Scripture Reading:*
> *Psalm 110, Psalm 100, Hebrews 7*

Psalm 110 is widely accepted as a messianic psalm, but this divinely inspired offering of David has been the source of scholarly debates. We'll explore the questions that scholars raise and the differing viewpoints. The richness of this chapter lies in not only the debate and discovery, but also the realization that God is intimately involved with our life here on earth. He isn't distant and uncaring. God has always planned eternity with us in mind. That should bring us hope today!

Much of the debate in Psalm 110 centers around the first verse:

> The LORD said to my Lord,
>   "Sit in the place of honor at my right hand
> until I humble your enemies,
>   making them a footstool under your feet."
>   (Psalm 110:1)

Scholars debate whether the New Testament Jesus is referenced in this psalm or God is having a conversation with another referred to as the Messiah or perhaps, humans.

You'll have an opportunity to process the differences in interpretation and I hope that you enjoy looking at the different perspectives. Not only that, but some of the questions that frame their debate have personal applications to your life and faith right now.

In this psalm, God speaks of the coming victory over enemies, but who is he talking to in this passage? Scholars debate on who God may be talking to, whether it's Jesus, Adam, Abraham, or even the prophet Elijah. As you learn and draw conclusions on your own of who's being addressed, the bottom line is that God guarantees his victory over the world, even in times of war.

> *God isn't afraid of questions. In fact, he invites them so that he can reveal more of himself to you.*

This is one of the times when it's good to give yourself the opportunity to get curious and to be open to learning. If you grew up in a religious tradition that shamed you or hushed you for having questions, you're in a safe space here. When I taught basic discipleship classes to new believers, I always told them, "Questions are welcomed! Meaningful debates are encouraged. I may not have all the answers, but rest assured, you aren't going to ask *the* question that will somehow undo God's sovereignty or disprove the Christian faith." I'd always sense a sigh of relief in the room. You've always got permission to ask questions and poke further. God isn't afraid of questions. In fact, he invites them so that he can reveal more of himself to you.

Is Jesus Actually in This Psalm?

Psalm 110 is one of the most often quoted scriptures in the New Testament. There are more than twenty direct and indirect references to this psalm. We'll explore specific examples after we tackle the bigger question of whether the messiah reference in this psalm pointed to Jesus. While looking at the psalm and taking it at face value, it seems that David is recording a celestial conversation between God and someone. That indication alone is spectacular. I mean, when's the last time that you overhead God talking to anyone? Let's not overlook the wow factor of that! During David's time, God's people didn't have the indwelling Holy Spirit or even their own personal copy of the scriptures. They did have certain men and women specifically assigned by God to be spokespersons or prophets. Contrary to some misunderstanding, prophets during Old Testament times did more than foretell elements of the future. They communicated what God wanted his people to know about him as well.

At the start of the chapter, I referenced Psalm 110:1. While you'll see other cross-references from Psalm 110 in the New Testament, let's start by looking specifically at several cross references to Psalm 110:1, which again says this:

> The LORD said to my Lord,
> "Sit in the place of honor at my right hand
> until I humble your enemies,
> making them a footstool under your feet."
> (Psalm 110:1)

First, David's confirmation as the author of Psalm 110 is confirmed by Jesus in Matthew 22 when he references this psalm while talking with religious leaders. The irony is that while Jesus confirms David's authorship, the question is whether David is talking about Jesus.

In Matthew 22, Jesus was approached by one group of religious leaders, the Sadducees, who asked Jesus a variety of questions hoping to trap him into heresy so that they could publicly discredit him. However, their attempts backfired because Jesus's answers impressed the crowd that had gathered to listen (Matthew 22:33). So, to pick up the baton dropped by the Sadducees, another set of religious leaders, the Pharisees, surrounded Jesus, ostensibly to pose their own tricky questions. However, Jesus tagged up first and asked them two questions in Matthew 22:42: *What do you think about the Messiah?* and *Whose son is he?*

The Pharisees answered that the Messiah was the son of David, but Jesus challenges them with one question that affirms David as the Spirit-led author of Psalm 110 as well as asks them an additional question that challenges their answer and renders them silent.

> Jesus responded, "Then why does David, speaking under the inspiration of the Spirit, call the Messiah 'my Lord'? For David said,
>
> > 'The LORD said to my Lord,
> > Sit in the place of honor at my right hand
> > until I humble your enemies beneath your feet.'
>
> "Since David called the Messiah 'my Lord,' how can the Messiah be his son?"
>
> No one could answer him. And after that, no one dared to ask him any more questions.
>
> (Matthew 22:43-46)

As Jesus begins his response, he notes that David is speaking under the inspiration of the Holy Spirit. This is important because no matter the debate about who God is speaking to in Psalm 110:1, the supernatural ability for David to hear and record such a conversation cannot be glossed over.

First, there are a lot of layers to how the Holy Spirit operated in the lives of individuals in the Old Testament, and while the Bible identifies the Holy Spirit's activity in certain individuals at certain times, it's completely possible that there are others who also experienced the indwelling presence for a certain purpose.[1]

Consider David's time in history. Practically speaking, how did he end up writing conversation between God and Jesus? It's not like he had a previous book from God to reference. The earliest writing paper and implements were available, but the Bible in the form that we have today was still more than a thousand years away. In fact, it would be around 250 CE before there was generally universal agreement around what's known as the "canon" or collection of Hebrew texts that comprise the Old Testament scriptures.[2]

David wasn't only a king, but also a prophet sent to speak for God to the people of Israel. Prophets declared God's word, but the emphasis of their message wasn't on predicting the future. One key piece of evidence that David served as a prophet of God is the sheer number of psalms attributed to him. However, if a prophet did speak about the future, their credibility rested on whether their foretelling was fulfilled (Deuteronomy 18:20-22).

Jesus knows that the religious leaders are out to get him, so he leads off with a stumper question: How could the Messiah be David's son? *Hint: Think Christmas.* Jesus had to come to earth from heaven in human form. This is known as the Incarnation. One scholar explains this whole scenario like this: "As eternal God, Jesus is the 'root [originator] of David,' and as a man, he is 'the offspring of David.' Had the Pharisees honestly faced this truth, they would have had to confess that Jesus is indeed the Son of God come in the flesh, but they refused to do so."[3]

As a cross-reference to Psalm 110:1, there are a lot of mentions of the word LORD, however, not all mentions are the same. Buckle up for a little Bible and translation history. But don't think seminary thick, but a rather easy-to-read, CliffsNotes version determines whom God is addressing in Psalm 110:1 and whether Jesus is the Messiah referenced in that verse.

So, what had happened was…

In Genesis 1:1, God's name is translated as the Hebrew word *Elohim*, meaning "God" or "divine."[4] However, God chooses a man named Moses to reveal himself to in the form of a burning bush. As God explains who he is and Moses's assignment to lead the Hebrew people out of slavery, Moses asks the name of the voice that is speaking to him. God's reply:

> "I AM WHO I AM." Say this to the people of Israel... Yahweh, the God of your ancestors—the God of Abraham, the God of Isaac, and the God of Jacob—has sent me to you.
>
> (Exodus 3:14-15)

It's here that God gives his sacred, holy name for the first time, *Yahweh*.[5] God's sacred, holy name appears around 6,000 times in the Old Testament. You may be wondering why your Bible doesn't use the word *Yahweh* as God's sacred, holy name. Non-Jewish, English translations do not use the word *Yahweh*, rather rendered as LORD.

At some point in late Old Testament times, the Jewish people believed that God's holy name was too sacred for them to say aloud. So, a few work-arounds were developed that eventually shaped how we see and read our Bible today.

The name *Yahweh* was written as YHWH (or yud-heh-vav-heh) and was meant to be unpronounceable. However, what could people say instead to acknowledge God with their lips? Enter the replacement word *Adonai*, meaning "Lord."[6] This Hebrew name for God became translated in the Greek version of the Old Testament as *kurios*, also given as *kyrios*.[7]

The evolution of the translated words that are associated with God's holy name continued. According to one source, when the Masoretes, a group of Jewish scribes in the fifth to tenth centuries CE, worked on translating the Hebrew Bible into Latin, they took the additional step of integrating the tetragrammaton (YHWH) with the vowels in *Adonai* and produced a Latin version of *Yahweh* known as *Jehowah*.[8] (If you're wondering why the vowels in *Adonai* don't exactly match up with the vowels in *Jehowah*, that's a matter of translation science between the Hebrew and Latin languages.) That word may look familiar to you, and it should. Eventually, the word was converted to what those familiar with the Bible and Christian faith know as *Jehovah*.

Now, this is where the difference of opinion arises in Psalm 110:1 as well as Matthew 22:44. As Jesus challenges religious leaders with the twister question, the twists and turns in the debate around who David refers to as the second *Lord* and the translation of the second reference to *Lord* continue.

Let's explore the two viewpoints on Psalm 110:1 and you can consider for yourself who God conversed with in this passage.

Viewpoint #1: God is not conversing with Jesus in Psalm 110:1.

In the Strong's Concordance, the Hebrew word associated with the second "Lord" in Psalm 110:1 is *ladoni*, which is used twenty-three times in the King James version of the Old Testament. The examples of *ladoni*,[9] like in Genesis 24:36, refer to a human master or authority figure, not a member from the Godhead. In fact, one source cites that Rabbinic tradition refers to *ladoni* as Abraham, not Jesus.[10]

> *And Sarah my master's wife bare a son to my master when she was old: and unto him hath he given all that he hath.*
>
> *(Genesis 24:36 KJV)*

Another opposing view asserted by a researcher is that based on the translation of *ladoni* and the portion of Psalm 110:1, when God tells "my Lord" to take a seat at his right hand, then Jesus isn't recognized as having equal authority or power. "God bestows his saving power on Christ," therefore denying that Jesus has the power to save, which would invalidate his claims to be God.[11] Extending that argument, those who don't believe that Jesus is referred to in Psalm 110:1 use Jesus's own words from John 6:38 where Jesus says that he came to do the will of God, not his own will:

> *For I have come down from heaven to do the will of God who sent me, not to do my own will.*
>
> *(John 6:38)*

Finally, the opposing viewpoint also cites that the Greek translations of *kurios* or *kyrios* as the Lord refers to Jesus with reverence, but not in the divine, trinitarian sense.

> *Therefore, since we have been made right in God's sight by faith, we have peace with God because of what Jesus Christ our Lord has done for us.*
>
> *(Romans 5:1)*

However, this argument only applies to certain uses of the Lord because there are other uses that are attributed to Jesus's divine nature, like Philippians 2:11:

> *and every tongue declare that Jesus Christ is Lord,*
> *to the glory of God the Father.*

In this instance, tracing the Greek roots of the word includes *master*, but also a title of honor as well as a name used for God.[12]

Viewpoint #2: God is conversing with Jesus in Psalm 110:1

The main support for championing the viewpoint that God is conversing with Jesus in Psalm 110:1 is found in New Testament scripture that not only references the Messiah, but specifically asserts Jesus as the Messiah. Here are a selection on cross-referenced verses. You'll pick up on their connection to the language in Psalm 110:1.

1. Peter Preaching the Gospel of Christ on the Day of Pentecost to Unbelievers:

    > *For David himself never ascended into heaven, yet he said,*
    >
    > *"The L*ORD* said to my Lord,*
    > *'Sit in the place of honor at my right hand*
    > *until I humble your enemies,*
    > *making them a footstool under your feet.'"*
    >
    > *(Acts 2:34-35)*

2. Paul writing to the Corinthian believers:

    > *For Christ must reign until he humbles all his enemies beneath his feet.*
    >
    > *(1 Corinthians 15:25)*

3. The writer of Hebrews asserting that Jesus was higher than the angels in heaven:

> *And God never said to any of the angels,*
>> *"Sit in the place of honor at my right hand*
>> *until I humble your enemies,*
>> *making them a footstool under your feet."*
>>> *(Hebrews 1:13)*

4. The writer of Hebrews details Jesus's once for all time sacrifice, and in this verse, the writer notes that Jesus sits at the right hand of God, not because he was commanded, but that he chose that place in the proximity of a holy, sovereign God:

> *There he waits until his enemies are humbled and made a footstool under his feet.*
>> *(Hebrews 10:13)*

When considering the position that Psalm 110 is a conversation between God and Jesus, you get to examine each viewpoint and decide for yourself. While you're weighing the opinions of both sides, let's explore the question that Jesus posed to the religious leaders in Matthew 22:42. It's a question that applies specifically to your life and mine each day as well as for our eternity: What do you think about the Messiah?

If you hold to the first viewpoint and the opinion that David recorded a conversation between God and Abraham or another human, then Psalm 110 may not rise to the level of a messianic psalm for you. However, removing a single psalm doesn't dismantle the rest of the evidence for Christ as Messiah that we will cover in this journey.

However, if you consider and agree with the assertion that David references Jesus as the Messiah, then what do you think of him? I lean toward the second viewpoint because for me the New Testament scriptural support is convincing, but I also acknowledge that some scholars, theologians, and you may disagree.

Like the ancient religious leaders, our world bristles at the idea of acknowledging the Messiah is Jesus and that Jesus is God of all. If we can intellectually or internally deny the divine supremacy of Christ, then we can see Jesus as a smart guy who was kind to people, but he has no authority in our lives. This means that we won't feel the need to be accountable to Jesus's teachings or truth. The reality is that if you acknowledge that Jesus is God and has authority over all, then everything will change, especially the things that you don't want to change. One writer summarized it like this: "The gospel is not only that Jesus is your Savior, but it's also that He's your Lord. This is about obedience. He not only gets to shape what you believe, He also gets to shape how you live."[13] Ultimately, if Jesus was the Messiah, that meant that the religious leaders would need to bow down before him. You too. In fact, me too. If there is a debate about Jesus and whether he is the second Person of the Godhead, then our world can put a pin in making a decision and continue to skip along our merry "I'll-do-it-my-way" rebellious way.

The reality is that if you acknowledge that Jesus is God and has authority over all, then everything will change, especially the things that you don't want to change.

Ultimately, you get to decide for yourself. In this unique season of looking at Jesus revealed in the Psalms, there are plenty of opportunities to talk with other believers and do some extra research and digging on your own.

For the remainder of the chapter, we will explore Psalm 110 as a conversation between God and the coming Messiah. I believe the scriptural evidence supports that this Messiah is Jesus Christ.

Feet Up in Place of Honor

Tackling the theology in the previous section was challenging, but the later portion of Psalm 110:1 contains one of my favorite examples of biblical imagery in scripture. David records God saying this to the Messiah, "until I humble your enemies, / making them a footstool under your feet."

Notice the visual imagery David writes about is how God will subjugate Jesus's enemies until they are low enough to be underfoot. Footstools maybe a practical piece of furniture, but they are also a symbol in scripture of a messianic promise repeated numerous times in the New Testament that God will humble anyone in opposition of Christ.

A similar scriptural analogy around humbling enemies was making the loser in an ancient battle and forcing him to the ground, whether face down or up so that the victor could put a foot (probably dirty and stinky) on their vulnerable neck. This was a final public humiliation before imprisonment or death.

One of my favorite Old Testament stories is when Joshua and the Israelites defeat a group of five kings in Canaan. Not only do the Israelite leaders get to place their feet on the defeated kings, but Joshua invites the soldiers do to the same (Joshua 10:24). It's one thing to imagine a world leader putting his or her foot across the neck of another world leader, but how wild would it be for a simple citizen to do the same?

Regardless of the footstool imagery or the symbolic act of placing a foot across the loser's neck, God's promise that the proud opposition against God will fall should evoke tremendous hope for us as well as a sobering moment of introspection. For those of us who proclaim faith in Jesus Christ, we take hope that in a world where for many, not just world leaders, who consider themselves outside of accountability or are filled with selfish or destructive pride, there will come a day when they kneel before Christ. For those who've wondered if God will make right the atrocities that unrepentant humans have inflicted, the answer is yes. There will come a day when those who've used their influence throughout human history to hurt, oppress, pervert, enslave, rob, torture, or any other form of evil will be humiliated and held to account.

Keep in mind, however, that defeated state they will face one day won't be because Jesus is subjugating them out of hate; rather, it will be because of their rejection of Jesus as the Lord and Savior of their lives. There is a sobering note to this. It won't be just the leaders who will be held accountable for their rejection of Jesus. Furthermore, it won't just be the openly evil or loudly hostile that will find themselves humbled, but anyone who lives in a pride that rebels against submitting to God.

As we point to various celebrities, tycoons, politicians, or world leaders who seem to reject God, we find that they aren't the only ones. This is hard to say, but nice, quiet, or unassuming everyday people also live with hearts closed off to God, even as they mow their lawns and pay their bills on time.

Even as we are confident that God will reckon those who reject him, there is a beautiful beginning for those of us who've declared our faith in Christ.

There's no timeline indicated in God's invitation as to when he will humble heaven's enemies, but until that day comes, we see how the resurrected Jesus's place is in the honored position. In scripture, there are various references to symbolism regarding the right position as an indicator of righteousness, or what aligns with God's holiness. Now, this is a good moment to slip on your Jesus glasses to avoid applying any American filters to any notions of right or left associated with politics or social issues. Our country has only been around for a few hundred years, so filtering God's character or sovereignty through our first-world, American perspective robs us of understanding the fullness of God. In plain language: Interpret scripture through "Jesus-glasses," not your American or your specific religious experience.

While the first verse of this chapter hopefully stoked your scriptural interest, there's more to learn in this chapter. Let's continue our review of Psalm 110.

God's Global Kingdom

*The LORD will extend your powerful kingdom from Jerusalem,
you will rule over your enemies.*

(Psalm 110:2)

At the time that David wrote this, Jerusalem was the center of life of the Israelite people. As you read Psalm 110:2, note that some translations use Zion rather than Jerusalem. Zion was the name of a fortress on a hill of the ancient city, Jebus, which would be later named Jerusalem. First Chronicles 11:4-9 records how David and the Israelites showed up in the land of the Jebusites, the original inhabitants of Jerusalem. The Jebusites taunted the Israelites because they believed that their fortress at Zion was impenetrable. But it wasn't. David and the Israelites captured the stronghold, and he renamed it The City of David. After conquering the fortress, David also expanded into the city and surrounding areas.

If you're familiar with the Old Testament, you know that David's kingdom would split apart after his son, King Solomon's death. After the split, both the Northern and Southern kingdoms of Israel would be conquered by other kingdoms and the Israelites would be held captive and ultimately released.

Centuries later, Jerusalem would be the location of Jesus's crucifixion and resurrection. While Jerusalem was under Roman rule, God's words in Psalm 110:2 foretold of a time when not only would Jerusalem regain its power, but that power would extend to all who were in opposition of Christ. In Revelation 21, the apostle John writes of a new Jerusalem from which God's glory would shine for eternity once all of the enemies of heaven are punished and all of God's promises to his people are fulfilled.

Won't He Do It!

*The LORD has taken an oath and will not break his vow.
"You are a priest forever in the order of Melchizedek."*

(Psalm 110:4)

There's a popular call-and-response that you might have heard in church depending on your background or familiarity with black church culture. It sounds like this:

> *Won't he do it?*
> *Won't he will?*

This call-and-response celebrates God's faithfulness. Still the English major part of me must defer to my cultural roots and overlook the clear grammar train wreck here. This call-and-response is a perfect setup for the remaining portion of Psalm 110 where God dictates what he will do. Once God makes a promise to do something, he will follow through.

Jesus would become our once and for all time mediator and sacrifice (Hebrews 10:10-14) for our sin, but before in David's time and for many centuries after, priests filled that function.

After the Israelites were freed from slavery in Egypt, God gave Moses the law at Mount Sinai, which outlined many aspects of religious and social life, but it also detailed the priesthood or the role of the individuals who would be the human liaisons between God and his people. Before Jesus came to usher in a direct connection to God, priests were a reminder that there was a gap between humanity's sinfulness and God's holiness and a mediator was needed to bridge that gap.

Out of the twelve tribes of Israel who heard God's law, the tribe of Levi was selected as the tribe that provided the priests. Not every Levite was a priest, but all priests during that time came from Levi. In fact, the first priest was Moses's brother, Aaron, a Levite (Exodus 29).

In ancient Israel, the high priest's role was not only to lead the people spiritually, but also, once a year, the high priest would atone for the sins of the people by going into a special place (Holy of Holies) in the tabernacle and later temple, to offer an animal sacrifice. While that sacrifice would atone for the sins of the people for a time, a high priest would repeat that sacrifice year after year

(Exodus 30:30). Not only that, but without the indwelling presence of the Holy Spirit to reshape heart attitudes or break patterns of inbred sin, the people, including the high priests themselves, had to rely upon the law to try to guide them in their relationship with God (Hebrews 5:1-4). The result was like a centuries-old Band-Aid on a stinking, festering wound of human sin and sinful behaviors that the high priests would reapply annually—and many of the priests' hands were filthy dirty too.

In the last chapter, we explored Psalm 23 and the necessity of us viewing ourselves as sheep in need of the care of a Great Shepherd. One of the hallmarks of a good shepherd was vigilance in watching out for the sheep and providing for them. Unfortunately, the people whom God put in charge of watching out for his people weren't doing a good job. While we're all responsible for our own decisions and behaviors, some of the struggles that we have with understanding what it means to have a personal connection with God have been influenced by the selfish, self-centered, or outright sinful religious leaders around us. In Jesus's time, the priests expanded their religious influence and held much political power. Not all the leaders of our faith fall into that category. As one who sits here today in tremendous gratitude for the lifetime of godly leaders who've been good shepherds to me, my heart breaks for those who have had poor or bad experiences. Again, we're responsible for our decisions and our own relationship with Christ, and at the same time, many of us are walking through the wake of former or current authority figures in our faith who have been bad shepherds in some form or another.

In Psalm 110:4 David writes of the Lord affirmed as a priest forever in the order of Melchizedek, described as the King of Salem in Genesis 14. This king appears without an origin story or lineage that's noted in scripture. After rescuing his nephew from marauding kings, Abraham has an interaction with Melchizedek, who blesses Abraham, but does not bestow the forever priesthood upon him. However, in Hebrews 5:10, the author of Hebrews cross-references Psalm 110:4 and writes that God affirmed Jesus as a forever, righteous priest.

Melchizedek is mysterious because not much is known about his life other than the few verses that we read in Genesis 14 and a few illuminating details in Hebrews 7, which retells the Genesis account. In order to understand why it matters that God would identify Jesus as a priest in the order of Melchizedek and not the Levites, the writer in Hebrews lets us in on a few fascinating details:

- The name *Melchizedek* means "king of justice."
- King of Salem means "king of peace" and Salem is a name considered identical to Jerusalem.[14]
- There is no record of Melchizedek's parents, ancestors, nor the beginning or end of his life.
- Perhaps the most telling statement is this at the end of Hebrews 7:3: "He remains a priest forever, resembling the Son of God."

While there are some who debate that Melchizedek may have been an imaginary character, an angel, or even Christ himself,[15] Hebrews 7:3 points to the fact that he was a real human who lived and modeled for us an early reflection of Christ centuries before Jesus would come to earth as human form. Not only that, but the meanings of Melchizedek's name mirrored the two visions for our hope that as believers we cling to today: justice and peace.

God never forgets about his promises to us, especially when the world gets confusing or our view of God gets clouded by our own problems, pain, or suffering. God never forgets His promises!

Just as God proclaims a day when evil will be held to account and peace will be eternally restored, Melchizedek is an early symbol of that promise. This should remind us that God never forgets about his promises to us, especially when the world gets confusing or our view of God gets clouded by our own problems, pain, or suffering. God never forgets His promises!

Jesus's Overcoming Is Coming

> *The Lord stands at your right hand to protect you.*
> *He will strike down many kings when his anger erupts.*
> *He will punish the nations*
>   *and fill their lands with corpses;*
>   *he will shatter heads over the whole earth.*
> (Psalm 110:5-6)

The remaining part of Psalm 110 casts a vision of what Jesus will do on our behalf:

- He will protect us;
- He will bring justice and punishment;
- He will be victorious.

As you read these "will" statements, I hope that you do so with joy and anticipation in your heart, especially if you're like me and are often wearied by the weight of the world. While we aren't the only humans in history to live through long seasons of perilous times, we do feel the slow burn of our scorching earth and hear the building groan of our humanity.

Which one of these is meaningful to you today? I'm going to go ahead and pick all three because that's where I'm at right now. If you read Psalm 110:5-6 in other translations, action verbs like "crush" and "shatter" are used to describe what Jesus will do to those who oppose him. (Emphasis added in the following verses.)

> *God brings the nations to justice,*
>   *piling the dead bodies,* ***crushing*** *heads throughout the earth.*
> (Psalm 110:6 CEB)

> *He will execute judgment among the nations,*
>   *filling them with corpses;*

> he will **shatter** chiefs
> over the wide earth.
> (Psalm 110:6 ESV)

> He will judge the nations, heaping up the dead
> and **crushing** the rulers of the whole earth.
> (Psalm 110:6 NIV)

I'm not one for any kind of bloodlust, but I am grateful that Jesus will punish those who are carrying on human history's too-long record of evil and pain. While it may take an unknown amount of time for us to see this come to pass—in fact, scholars point to the final battle of Armageddon as the final fulfillment of these words[16]—we can believe that one day it will happen and as believers in Christ, we will see it, whether we're still living on earth or we witness it from eternity in heaven.

Knowing what Jesus will do—and that in the end, he will be victorious—is my only hope these days in a world where I choose not to own a television because there's so much pain and sadness in my own circle of connections, I made the decision to be mindful about how much of the world I allow to overwhelm my heart at any one time.

In the battle against evil, no human, not even a big screen, imagined Marvel Avenger can fight alone against epic evil. As humans, we face evil every single day. Sadly, on any given day, the consensus around our world is that evil is winning. Whether you're looking at the news, tough situations within your family, or perhaps even your own life, the epic battle of good versus evil plays out on small and grand scales each day. However, the evil that we see in our world isn't the full story of the evil that we're fighting.

There is a fight, in fact a multi-faceted war, that is rooted in an unseen spiritual world and manifests itself in the sadness, pain, horror, and death that we see in our world. In Psalm 110:5-6, David writes about the defeat of the type of evil that Paul describes to the Ephesian believers.

There's a spiritual battle far too much for us. Yet, not for God.

For those who believe that God is speaking to a human figure like David, then the verse reads like God will be right by humanity's side to defend and defeat the enemy. For those who see Psalm 110 as a conversation between God and Jesus the Messiah, this passage can be seen as the Lord, which is translated *adonay*[17] in this verse, is standing at the right hand of Jesus. If you recall, Psalm 110:1 refers to Jesus sitting at the right hand of God, and now, it can be inferred that God is at the right hand of Jesus.

Considering these verses reminds me of Jesus's words declared right before he was crucified. As you read this verse, consider the final sentence intentionally. I don't know what is happening in your life these days, but this message may specifically be for you.

> I have told you all this so that you may have peace in me. Here on earth you will have many trials and sorrows. But take heart, because I have overcome the world.
>
> (John 16:33)

When I look at John 16:33 through the reflection of Psalm 110:5-6, there's a specific description of how Jesus will overcome and how he's doing it in triune cooperation with God. Jesus declares that he has overcome the world. That's a declaration of divinity that is spoken for our comfort and most of all, our hope.

Knowing what Jesus will do—and that in the end, he will be victorious—is my only hope these days in a world filled with pain and sadness. I have made the decision to be mindful about how much of the world I allow to overwhelm my heart at any one time.

Finding Jesus as Our Hope

At the time I'm writing this, a beautiful young woman that I watched grow up with my own kids cradles her infant son as his tiny little body fights stage three liver cancer. The diagnosis was a rude sucker punch. Not just because a five-month-old baby shouldn't be diagnosed with cancer, but also because she survived her own cancer journey four years ago. There's an ache in my soul for her and her husband. The happy innocence of learning how to be parents has been ripped away and replaced with hospital stays, tears, prayers, and at times, suffocating uncertainty.

You aren't alone if you've looked at the world and declared that it's all too much.

Too much pain.

Too much heartbreak.

Too much sadness.

In this moment, I want to make room for you to look at your own "too much." It may be a past or present circumstance that crouches in the corner of your soul oozing anger or tears over what can't be fixed or changed. It might even be the thing that you hold in your hands and it keeps you from wholeheartedly holding onto God. For me, I've got two situations that right now fall into the "too much" category. They are near to my heart and in a naked moment of pure candor, spots where fear can flame up quickly if I'm not careful.

What's yours?

Now, for a moment, can I ask you to imagine placing it in Jesus's victorious hands as we close out our experience with Psalm 110? Jesus is our hope in our world today.

One of the reasons I want to invite you to step into this fresh hope is because we have the privilege of experiencing a personal relationship with God. Unlike the people before who relied on the priests, you and I can talk to God at anytime and anywhere. Not only that, but for the places where you just can't, God's Spirit lives within you, giving you the strength so that you can live the Christian life. Rather than allowing us to flounder and flop about on our own, God's Holy Spirit permanently lives within us, guiding us, equipping us, transforming us, and supernaturally enabling us to understand God's messages to us.

One of the ways that God's Holy Spirit invites us toward God is by encouraging us to praise God. We elevate what or whom we celebrate!

With that in mind, I want to conclude our time with Psalm 110 by asking you to reflect also on Psalm 100, which is a psalm of giving thanks. In light of God's message through David in Psalm 110, we have a lot to be thankful to God for. As you read, allow yourself to remember why it is that you are grateful to God and what he has done for you. This is a wonderful way to honor God as well as uplift your own heart today!

> Shout with joy to the LORD, all the earth!
> > Worship the LORD with gladness.
> > Come before him, singing with joy.
>
> Acknowledge that the LORD is God!
> > He made us, and we are his.
> > We are his people, the sheep of his pasture.
>
> Enter his gates with thanksgiving;
> > go into his courts with praise.
> > Give thanks to him and praise his name.
>
> For the LORD is good.
> > His unfailing love continues forever,
> > and his faithfulness continues to each generation.
>
> (Psalm 100)

SPIRITUAL JOURNEY REFLECTION

Using the following rubric: Red Light, Yellow Light, or Green Light, how do you see yourself in each of these three areas in the past week. *Remember: Be kind to yourself.*

- **Spiritual Attitude:** *What is your level of connection with God or willingness to live for eternal priorities?*
- **Spiritual Behavior:** *What do your normal actions or activities indicate about your level of obedience or surrender to God?*
- **Spiritual Character:** *How often do you present yourself to be Spirit-led, or when does your internal or external life look like Jesus?*

CHAPTER FIVE

Finding Jesus as Our Strength

CHAPTER FIVE
Finding Jesus as Our Strength

Scripture Reading:
Psalm 69, Matthew 26, John 18

One of my favorite sections in any movie is often found in the inspirational montage. This is the part of the movie where numerous scenes are edited together to show a lot of action and events happening in a short period of time. The fancy cinematic term for this is called the *Soviet Montage Theory*. The most popular example of this theory is the training scene from the movie *Rocky IV*. (Even though the movie was partially filmed in the former Soviet Union, that isn't the reason for the name.)

During the US/Soviet tensions in the '80s, Rocky Balboa travels across the world to train on a remote farm in the USSR. His previous boxing rival turned friend, Apollo Creed, was dead and Rocky was now preparing to fight Drago, the man who killed him. As multiple, quick movie scenes flash before the audience, Rocky trains for the fight of his life with crude tools like large rocks and an ancient wooden wagon and by running in hiking boots in the snow. His competitor, Drago, trains in a high-tech, sterile, and steroid-enabled environment. After seeing all of the clips of different scenes, a climactic moment happens when Rocky reaches his training goals and he runs up a mountain, climbing, clawing his way to the top, in stark contrast to his foe, and yells "Drago" over and over into the wind.

When we watch those inspirational montage scenes, the quick progression of the different images can make us forget the real-time realities that we face. Our struggles in life aren't solved in the same time frame, and any kind of mental transformation that we undergo takes a lot longer than a one- to two-minute training montage, even though we wish real transformation was that easy!

Yet, the importance of the preparation phase, especially the underdog moments, cannot be diminished, especially the journey to the scene of a final showdown.

This week, we're going to look at a low time in King David's life that corresponds to a deep and difficult time in Jesus's life shortly before he was nailed to the cross. While the world would look down with pity on their emotional condition, I pray that you would find encouragement and inspiration by seeing their vulnerability and their steadfast faith in God.

God, I Could Use Little Help Here (Psalm 69:1-3)

Psalm 69 is a highly emotional piece by King David written at an unclear time in his life. However, it has significant, direct connections between his experience and what Jesus would encounter centuries later at the time of his dramatic crucifixion, which we will look at in detail in the final chapter as we look at Psalm 22.

Upon reading the first three verses of Psalm 69, it takes no imagination to see that David is in a bad place here.

> Save me, O God,
>   for the floodwaters are up to my neck.
> Deeper and deeper I sink into the mire;
>   I can't find a foothold.

Finding Jesus as Our Strength

I am in deep water,
  and the floods overwhelm me.
I am exhausted from crying for help;
  my throat is parched.
My eyes are swollen with weeping,
  waiting for my God to help me.

Perhaps you've cried, begged, or gritted out that opening prayer: *Save me, O God.* It's a four-word plea that I've cried out many times and on many occasions. In fact, it crossed my lips just last week.

God isn't looking for eloquence or length when it comes to our prayers.

One of the comforts that I often find in reading scripture is when I see how great men and women of God find themselves in dire straits and utter the same kind of simple appeal to God that I pray when I'm overwhelmed. I've heard it said that "help" is a complete four-letter prayer. God isn't looking for eloquence or length when it comes to our prayers. As a longtime Bible study teacher and group leader, I've asked a lot of people why praying is challenging for them, especially in front of a group. Many cite a lack of confidence in what to say as well as a fear of saying the wrong words or combination of words. Yet, David's "Save me, O God!" demonstrates two principles of what I call "good and gritty prayers": *short and honest.* Keep that in mind next time if your desire to pray starts getting hijacked by any fear of praying. Go for short and honest and get that prayer out there to God!

David appeals to God because he is in some type of predicament and can't save himself. He uses floodwaters as imagery to describe the big, complicated, and confusing rushing and swirling through his life. Not only that but he also describes his emotional state as sinking in the mud. This is a one-two punch of someone who's having a really hard time and doesn't have the energy to make it better. It's one thing if a person in a flood can grab onto a piece of debris floating by or cling to a tree on the edge of the waters, but if someone is sinking while the violent waters are rushing, well, that's feels daunting. It's one thing to feel your reasons for hoping diminishing, but the danger comes when one feels hopeless, like sinking with no hope of rescue.

As Psalm 69:3 begins, *hopeless* describes David's state as he details his exhausted tears and swollen eyes. However, there is a glimmer of hope as David ends his description of suffering by proclaiming that he is waiting for his God to help him.

While I have never been in a flash flood or faced down the rushing water from a busted levee, I did get stranded on top of my little brown 1984 Chevette when I was a senior in high school. I was on my way to a band performance during a severe thunderstorm when the street that I was driving down began to flood and I had no way out. As I sat on top of my little car and watched the water rise, I kept looking for someone to see me and come to save me. This was at a time before cell phones, so I had to wait for someone to come out of their home and offer to call my dad on their home phone. I can't tell you the relief that I experienced as I saw my dad's giant white truck drive up over the hill in the distance. By that point, the floodwaters were as high as the window opening of my little car. But Dad's truck had really tall tires, so he could drive pretty deep into the flooded waters to pluck me off the top of my car roof.

As you've learned more about David's life in previous chapters, it's not hard to imagine that he was facing dire circumstances that would prompt his four-word prayer. In fact, David renews this "Save me, O God" refrain a few verses later in Psalm 69:13-18. While his prayer expands to more specific prayer requests like "take care of me," "come and redeem me," and "free me," the fact remains that David's difficulties stacked higher than the top of his royal crown. David had people-problems, political-problems, and at times, pride-problems that created a snowball of consequences

Finding Jesus as Our Strength

for himself and others. He's people like us, isn't he? In fact, these verses mirror another set of verses in Isaiah that I've read countless times myself:

> When you go through deep waters,
>   I will be with you.
> When you go through rivers of difficulty,
>   you will not drown.
>
> (Isaiah 43:2)

Stop and savor those words for a moment, especially if you've been praying "Save me, O God" lately. Notice the difference between deep waters and rivers of difficulty. I see deep waters as those overwhelming circumstances that you may feel will take you out once and for all. But they won't because God's righteous right hand will hold you up. Then, the rivers of difficulty look like those long-term situations like chronic illnesses, estranged relationships, a tough marriage, or troubled children. These are the ongoing life struggles where you've got to swim through each day, one continual stroke after another. Some days, you're not sure if you can keep going. It's normal if you've wanted to give up or the exhaustion starts messing with your mind. Know this: God assures you that you can make it.

Take a deep breath.
Remember God's promises to you.
Do the next right thing.

I hope that God's reassurance to you in Isaiah 43:2 lifts your spirits, especially if you can relate to David's sense of sinking. I also find comfort in the fact that Jesus also battled through a similarly low moment in his life, yet he models exactly what we need to do to find the hope and help that we need.

In Matthew 26, Jesus expresses a similar sentiment as David just before getting arrested. He was praying in the garden of Gethsemane with the disciples, sans Judas, after the Passover meal. For those who love background Bible facts, the garden of Gethsemane is often identified as an olive grove by scholars even though the location of the garden isn't exactly known.[1] Jesus would often go to this garden with the disciples (John 18:2). They were surrounded by olive trees and likely an olive press, a place where olives were crushed to release the oils, which would be used as "fuel for lamps (Exodus 27:20), as anointing oil (Leviticus 2:1)...and for dressing wounds (Luke 10:34)."[2] Each of these products came as a result of the olives crushing and they connect to symbols attributed to Jesus and his character such as "his life brought light to everyone" (John 1:4). As the prophet wrote, Jesus would be "crushed for our sins" (Isaiah 53:5).

No one, not even Jesus, would look forward to being crushed. The record in Matthew 26 reflects Jesus's "Save me, O God" prayer. First, Jesus mirrors David's emotional pain in Matthew 26:37b-38: "he became anguished and distressed. He told them [the disciples], 'My soul is crushed with grief to the point of death. Stay here and keep watch with me.'"

Jesus may have been determined, but he wasn't hardened against the reality that he'd be facing. He didn't turn off his emotions and go numb. He was real about how he felt to the people closest to him. Sit with Jesus's words for a moment. He said that his soul was crushed with a grief so intense if felt like he was being suffocated to death by it. One scholar observes "Jesus's sorrow resulted from his anticipation of his physical, emotional, and spiritual suffering, especially his alienation from his Father as he bore the sins of the world on the cross."[3]

This is the point at which I encounter some inner conflict that I must be careful not to turn into a point of guilt or condemnation. Whereas David was experiencing dire circumstances that prompted him to call out to God, Jesus's distress was part of the setup for our salvation. It's overwhelming to think about Jesus looking at the remnants of crushed bits and pieces of olives scattered on the ground knowing that his body would be ripped and torn apart before dying. Yet, Jesus was committed to that which he told the Father that he would do.

David's People Problems
(Psalm 69:4)

Those who hate me without cause
  outnumber the hairs on my head.
Many enemies try to destroy me with lies,
  demanding that I give back what I didn't steal.
                              (Psalm 69:4)

One solitary verse, Psalm 69:4, paints a broad picture of David's people problems. Again, it's not completely clear at which point David is writing these words. In fact, one commentary points to Psalm 69:35 and questions whether this verse was written later, like during the lifetime of Jeremiah when the Israelites were released from exile, which occurred many years after David's death.[4]

Regardless of timeline, David laments not just that he's got enemies, but he's got a lot of enemies gunning for him unjustly. (Okay, so they didn't have guns back then, but you get the drift.) Since he was a public personality, there were a lot of reasons why he'd have a lot of enemies.

I remember working in one environment where another person on my team just didn't like me. Even when we sat down in my office to air out the matter, she couldn't point to a reason why she didn't like me; just my communication style, mannerisms, and overall general vibe grated on her. For a while, I attempted to win her over. However, striving to change her opinion of me consumed a valuable chunk of my energy each day. I wore myself out being overly cautious about every single word that I said to her, even though I had always been pleasant before. It wasn't until after she left our office that I realized that I was never going to win her over. I gave up my peace over trying to change her opinion when I should have accepted it and focused on my own business.

David bemoans paying a price for problems that he didn't cause. In 2 Samuel 16, there's a man named Shimei who was related to the former King Saul, who'd died in battle. Shimei carried a grudge against now King David. Shimei throws rocks at David and his entourage while screaming that David was a murderer and scoundrel. That's awkward, right? Imagine how David must have felt as Shimei yelled insults while the other Israelites came out of their houses and, no doubt, heard it all. Shimei claimed that David stole King Saul's throne and that God would take revenge on David for the bloodshed (2 Samuel 16).

David's military men wanted to kill Shimei for his physical and verbal assault, but David gives us insight into his humble human heart. In verses 11-12, David reflects on how his own son is trying to kill him so it's not completely out of bounds that one of Saul's relatives might have a beef with him. He doesn't take Shimei's insults personally—a lesson that we can tuck away for ourselves. One of my favorite slogans that I learned years ago is *QTIP: Quit Taking It Personally*. It's a mental and emotional tool that I use as a boundary to keep me from getting caught up in the opinions of others.

At the end of his encounter with Shimei, David hopes that God will see the wrong judgments against David and bless him for it one day. David told his soldiers to leave the angry man alone, even though his curses and rock throwing did exhaust them to the point at which they needed to stop and rest by the Jordan River (2 Samuel 16). I don't know why this detail was added to the end of the story, but it is a good reminder that dealing with people problems will wear us out. When I'm in seasons where interpersonal conflict is high with one person, I add relational ballast to my life by intentionally scheduling fun or meaningful time with two friends.

I don't know if that was one of the memories that came to mind while David wrote Psalm 69:4, but perhaps you can relate to David's encounter with the angry Shimei. Who are the Shimeis in your life? They are the people who should know better about you, but they ignore who you are in favor of what they want to think. It's so frustrating when you're trying to do your best to love Jesus and love others, but certain people just don't like you.

Jesus understands. Imagine how he would have felt in the garden of Gethsemane, after praying many times for God to provide another way that would release him from pain and suffering. As I wrote previously, Jesus prayed not once or twice, but three times for God to take his cup of suffering away, yet Jesus stood by his intention to do God's will (Matthew 26:39-42).

When Judas showed up later with the religious leaders as well as a group of Roman soldiers and temple guards, many carrying blazing torches and weapons, Jesus knew that the time had come. He'd done nothing wrong, but they came for him anyways. Jesus could have invoked the power of heaven to make his enemies go away, but he didn't. However, there was a glimpse into what could have happened if he had.

> *Jesus fully realized all that was going to happen to him, so he stepped forward to meet them. "Who are you looking for?" he asked.*
>
> *"Jesus the Nazarene," they replied.*
>
> *"I AM he," Jesus said. (Judas, who betrayed him, was standing with them.) As Jesus said "I AM he," they all drew back and fell to the ground!*
>
> John 18:4-6

Whereas David didn't have the power to stop his enemies that unjustly accused him, Jesus did have the power, but he didn't use it. Yet, we can see the evidence of that power and it's more than stunning.

Notice, all Jesus must do is speak his divine name and that entire contingent of religious leaders, Roman soldiers, and temple guards were pushed back and fell to the ground. I imagine that it felt like the power of a bomb blast that rocked them from their feet. I would have loved to have seen that!

And in another example of Jesus's face set like flint with determination, notice how once Jesus realized everything that would happen, he didn't take a step back and hesitate; the scriptural author writes, "he stepped forward to meet them."

Just as David overlooked the insults and painful disdain of Shimei, Jesus did not let the angry mob deter him from his purpose.

Unashamed and Forgiven
(Psalm 69:5)

David wasn't fake. He didn't pretend to be better than what he was. There were times when he succumbed to sin or turned his head in denial, but he gives us a master class in how to be real before God while not trashing himself in a way that undermined how God saw him.

In verse 5, David's candor is refreshing, especially as so many Christians were criticized for being fake or hypocritical because they pretend that they don't have struggles or sin. I don't know about you, but I'm drawn to people who are courageous enough to be real about their flaws.

> O God, you know how foolish I am;
> my sins cannot be hidden from you.
> (Psalm 69:5)

There's a humility in David's confession that is both admirable and, at least for me, uncomfortable. Of all the ways that we prefer to describe ourselves, "foolish" usually doesn't make the cut. Yet, David never loses sight of God's supernatural wisdom as compared to David's best human thinking. For the times when David tried to skim his sin over with silence, he paid a hefty internal price.

> **One of the opportunities that the Lenten season creates is a chance at renewed communication with God.**

Is there a sin that you've never spoken to God about? I want to tread tenderly here, recognizing that there may be a great deal of guilt, shame, or fear that screams for you to stay silent. But, what if you could finally experience freedom and forgiveness on the other side? One of the opportunities that the Lenten season creates is a chance at renewed communication with God. Could this be the time when you tell God about whatever it is that's been on your heart for far too long? It will be hard, but here's what happened when David confessed his sin:

> Finally, I confessed all my sins to you
>   and stopped trying to hide my guilt.
> I said to myself, "I will confess my rebellion to the LORD."
>   And you forgave me! All my guilt is gone.
> (Psalm 32:5)

I've experienced the joy and clear conscience that comes after confession. Ahhhh, there's nothing like the feeling of the dead weight of guilt and shame getting peeled off by God once I confess to Him. Too often, we convince ourselves that it's easier to live with the guilt or the shame, even though we're miserable. Without releasing the truth to God, the guilt and shame manifest as heavy weights of self-defeating thoughts or self-sabotaging behavior. That weight presses down, heavier and heavier until a person feels buried under the weight, squeezing out all hope, joy, and peace. If you can relate, there's good news for you today.

Let God lift the weight today. Right here, right now is a chance for you to initiate the journey of forgiveness and freedom. You take the first step and God will help you.

The first step is admitting that you need to confess. The Lenten season is a great time to make a clean start in your faith. The next step is the one where you may have gotten stuck. This is the place where you talk to God. If you need words, you can use the prayer on the next page. I've also added in some spaces for you to personalize your conversation with God. You don't need to make this fancy and don't let your emotions control your confession. If you are ready to confess, do it, even if you aren't sure what to do after your confession. God will take care of that.

Dear God, today, I want to confess _____ to you. I do not want to feel the guilt or shame any longer.

You promised in 1 John 1:9 that when I confess my sins, you will forgive me. I acknowledge that there is no sin that you won't forgive if I confess with a sincere heart.

God, I accept your forgiveness. I pray that you remove the feelings of guilt and shame over _____ so that I can enjoy your freedom and the peace of a clear conscience before you.

Help me to understand your next steps for me so that I can continue to experience your ultimate healing and freedom.

In Jesus's name, Amen.

God never expects you to live a perfect life, but you need his forgiveness to live a peaceful life. We all make mistakes, even mature believers. I pray that you always have David's heart and humble attitude when it involves not hiding your sin or your struggles from God. His dream for you is to experience the grace and the peace that Jesus died to bring so that you live in freedom, both as a blessing from God as well as a way to inspire others to draw near to God as well.

A Good Reason *Not* to Care What Others Think (Psalm 69:6-12)

In our world today, being a follower of Jesus Christ isn't easy. In today's time, it's no secret that Christianity has lost its once esteemed, respected place in culture. In a recent study, only 26% of millennials had a very positive view of Christianity. They also rely less on the Bible as a guide for moral decisions with 63% choosing to "lean on personal emotions, past experiences, and the advice of other people." For those who think that the younger generation would be fine if they'd just get back into church, the study reported that millennials trust pastors less than other trust-based roles like elected officials, celebrities, journalists, or influencers (54% versus 57% respectively).⁵

Just as David's zeal for God invited the negative attention of others, we sometimes experience the same. Yet, as David recounts his fasting, times of repentance, and his trust in God he doesn't let the treatment of others stop him. In verse 12, David knows that the drunks sing about him, making fun of him. This is quite a sobering testimony from a man who sits on a royal throne.

David's pleas about not being put to shame for trusting God are echoed in several places in scripture. At various times, God gives us reassurance that our decision to follow him is the right decision even if our world yells that we're making the wrong decision, like forgiving those who hurt us or obeying God when it would easier to just do what everyone else is doing.

As you thought about the last few weeks or months of your daily Christian life, when are the times that you've felt tension in standing up for your faith? Perhaps it was the time when you shared a Bible verse on your social media and noticed that your funny meme post got a lot more attention. Maybe you were talking with your coworkers and sharing a funny story from your small group gathering the night before and noticed a few raised eyebrows when you mentioned that you went to a Bible study group. For some of you, it's your Christian beliefs that make you stand out against the landscape of the cultural status quo when it comes to dating standards, tithing, praying in public, or business practices. Whether you are the only one living like Jesus in your environment or it just feels like it because others aren't ready to make themselves known, God sees your courage. It matters.

Throughout the years of Jesus's public ministry, he was often criticized and challenged by religious leaders as well as those who gathered in the crowds to hear him. We've covered a few instances where Jesus was directly confronted by religious leaders who wanted to trap him into making statements that would be contrary to the law so that they could arrest him. However, Jesus saw all of those traps coming.

Jesus upset both the religious and cultural status quo. He invited men like Matthew to follow him even though the Jewish community despised tax collectors. Jesus made connections with unnamed men and women from all walks of life and he healed them. Not only that, I love that Jesus invited women to be a part of his ministry whereas religious leaders would sometimes ignore even their wives and daughters in public. During all the criticism, Jesus continued to live out the mission that God called him to do.

Does Anyone Care About Me? (Psalm 69:19-21)

David revisits some of his expressed sadness in the earlier verses. Now, we see David taking his enemy's actions personally. This is a rare kind of vulnerability that we often do not see from those in leadership, and I don't know about you, but I find it highly admirable. Even as David sits on a high throne, he still has a heart that can be broken.

David is self-aware enough to know that he is the cause of some of his pain. However, as a king, David sees the vast army of enemies around him, and at the point in the life that he is writing, it seems to be that he doesn't have a support system to help him. David's words reflect the deep sense of loneliness that an increasing number of people in our world, perhaps even you, feel today:

> *If only one person would show some pity;*
> *if only one would turn and comfort me.*
> (Psalm 69:20b)

David's words remind me of the various celebrities who write memoirs or tragically leave suicide letters. Many of them talk about the loneliness of being surrounded by so many but still feeling unseen and unknown, only wanted for what they can buy or the doors that they can open for others. Perhaps that's how David felt. As king, he would have been extremely popular with those who wanted to build their own careers or use his name for their gain. But it seems that at a time when David felt that so many were against him, he didn't feel as if anyone was for him.

You don't have to be a king to relate. Hopefully, you do have a circle of community around you. Maybe, if you don't have a circle of community, you have at least one person that you can reach out who will listen when you are having a hard time.

Affirming that this isn't the case for David, he points out that he can't count on anyone around him to care for him, even saying that they would give him poison for food and sour wine for his thirst. The word for poison is also referred to as *gall*, a poisonous herb. I mean, if you show up at a friend's house for dinner and a pile of gall is on the plate, that lets you know right there that you aren't on the same level of friendship as you'd thought.

It's here that we can feel both sympathy and empathy for David. Sympathy that the man after God's own heart finds himself isolated and alone against a legion of enemies. Also, empathy because many of us have felt the same at different times in our lives.

Years ago, I remember having a conversation with someone who'd finally spoken up and called attention to another family member's inappropriate touching. Not only did my acquaintance's parents deny the report, but many family members took sides against this person, squeezing them out of their relational circle. While not completely banishing the individual, there was a frosty chill line that communicated that the person was no longer welcome if they continued to stand up for that story. At holidays and special days, this individual grieves the loss of connection and the continuing sting of rejection.

While it's difficult to share stories like those, my friend's story communicates the gravity and pain of isolation, especially through no fault of one's own. David understood this. Jesus understood it as well.

In the next chapter, we will take an in-depth look into Psalm 22, which covers the striking and stunning details of Jesus's crucifixion.

However, there is an overlap in Psalm 69:21. David's experience in being offered gall for food and sour wine for thirst mirrors the experience of Jesus as he is on the cross. At one point, he is offered and denies the sour drink as well.

Still Giving Thanks
(Psalm 69:30-33)

In many of David's difficult, emotional psalms, he winds down his writings pointing toward the positive. In Psalm 69:30-33, David affirms that he will continue to praise God and give him thanks. This is an important part of David's character that we can't overlook. Remember, at the beginning of the chapter he felt as if he was drowning in the floodwaters while hopelessly sinking into the mud. That's usually not a place in life that prompts one to feel overly thankful. But David chooses to give thanks anyways.

What would it look like for you to give thanks to God today even though your circumstances and perhaps even your outlook on life feel hopeless? In the New Testament, the apostle Paul encourages us to maintain a prayerful way of life and to give thanks always (1 Thessalonians 5:18). The call to give thanks isn't for God's sake; it's for ours. When we give thanks to God, it gets us out of our own heads and agendas, disrupting our circuitry of sadness and allowing us to connect God's promises with his faithfulness in our lives. Giving thanks to God is more beneficial for you spiritually than your religious determination to try to be a good Christian. In giving thanks, you take the time to see where God is at work and active in your life.

In giving thanks, you take the time to see where God is at work and active in your life.

There is a humility that David identifies that comes with giving thanks that can protect us from running along self-interested paths that can lead us away from the life-giving connection and help that we absolutely need from God. One of my favorite portions in this section is from verse 32: "Let all who seek God's help be encouraged."

In my opinion, verse 33 is a prophetic verse that connects David's writing to the reason why God sent Jesus to save us: "For the LORD hears the cries of the needy; / he does not despise his imprisoned people."

God knew that we needed to be rescued from the imprisonment and death sentence associated with sin. While scripture records the faults and failures of many, at the heart of it all is humanity's deep need to be rescued from our sinful nature. God heard that cry as he looked upon the tragedy that humanity had brought upon itself. He saw the brokenness, the destruction, and the desperate need that the people had to be saved from their own sinful desires.

Jesus moved toward the cross for our freedom. Even as he stood in that garden and allowed his heart to bear its true emotion, he was not shaken from his purpose. Jesus knew that our freedom couldn't be brought any other way and he loved us enough to win that freedom for us.

Praising God for Eternity (Psalm 69:34-36)

David lived in an ancient time before cell phones, online shopping, and driverless cars, yet he could still write under the inspiration of the Holy Spirit to proclaim God's plans for his people.

In the closing of Psalm 69, David calls for God's people to praise God for rescuing, rebuilding, and redeeming Jerusalem. During David's time as king, Israel is united. However, in various prophetic visions previously mentioned, God lets David know that it won't always be that way.

In the near future, the Israelites will be taken into the Babylonian captivity for approximately seventy years. After that, they will rebuild Jerusalem, the temple, and their lives until another invasion by Alexander the Great. Centuries later, Herod would rebuild the temple in Jerusalem and the Romans would destroy it again in 70 CE. Not only that, but the Israelites would suffer and be subjugated to various emperors, kings, persecution, and ridicule. This is hardly the future that King David wanted for his people.

But God had something better planned. While he didn't give David details, he does give the man after his own heart a glimpse of it.

The ending verses of this psalm paint a prophetic outline filled in a little more by John in Revelation 21 as he writes about the New Jerusalem as well as the new heaven and new earth. For all that God restores, he also removes, "He will wipe every tear from their eyes, and there will be no more death or sorrow or crying or pain. All these things are gone forever" (Revelation 21:4).

Even as David cries out to God for rescue at the beginning of this chapter, the end of this chapter and, in fact, the end of our human story conclude with the victory that includes not only a God who brings his people to an eternal home that can never be ripped away, but he also brings lasting peace and security.

Living in our world isn't easy these days. Yet, we've got God's promised future ahead of us. Even on the difficult days when we cry out, "Save me, O God," He is there to keep us, hold us, and save us. While there will always be those who discourage us or try to defeat us, God's righteous right hand holds us above the angry waves and words.

May we follow in David's faithful words and continue to praise God, honor him, and thank him for all that he has done for us.

SPIRITUAL JOURNEY REFLECTION

Using the following rubric: Red Light, Yellow Light, or Green Light, how do you see yourself in each of these three areas in the past week. *Remember: Be kind to yourself.*

- **Spiritual Attitude:** *What is your level of connection with God or willingness to live for eternal priorities?*
- **Spiritual Behavior:** *What do your normal actions or activities indicate about your level of obedience or surrender to God?*
- **Spiritual Character:** *How often do you present yourself to be Spirit-led, or when does your internal or external life look like Jesus?*

CHAPTER SIX

Finding Jesus as Our Savior

CHAPTER SIX
Finding Jesus as Our Savior

> Scripture Reading:
> Psalm 22, Matthew 27, John 20

As we near the end of our time exploring Jesus in the Psalms, we'll conclude with, what's arguably the most well-known messianic poem, Psalm 22. It has a vibe that feels like a timeslip novel. This popular literary genre features a shared circumstance that unfolds in the past in one way while simultaneously unfolding in the future in a completely different way. As we've found Jesus in the psalms, either through symbolism or prophetic insight, it's fascinating to see the different layers and overlaps between David's life and words and Jesus's time on earth.

David's words in Psalm 22 contain words and imagery that closely pattern after Jesus's words, emotions, and suffering on the cross. David's tone vacillates between hopeless moments and a hopeful, eternal perspective. However, the latter portion of David's psalm erupts into a joyous chorus that sounds like the celebration we sing on Resurrection Sunday, complete with renewed tones of hope of grace, healing, and redemption.

Before you read David's words, consider whether you need to cleanse your Psalm 22 or crucifixion palette. If you already think that you know everything that you need to know or if you're feeling somewhat indifferent to the raw emotions that David expresses in this psalm, know that's a clue that you may need to invite God in to refresh your engagement and understanding. Prayer is the first step.

God, open my eyes to see David's words and Jesus's experience with fresh eyes so that I can understand your love and your grace in greater and deeper ways. Amen.

Shifting Your Perspective on the Crucifixion

When I was a church staffer, the discussion around Jesus's crucifixion was at times alarmingly impersonal. I led the spiritual growth and development team and we spent months getting ready for the handoff from our pastor and the weekend planning team that worked hard to create an engaging Easter experience for our attendees. Around our planning table and in our emails, Jesus was already down off the cross, in and out of the grave, and ascended to heaven before we got to Palm Sunday. The hurried rhythm of ministry caused us to take the cross for granted. While our intentions were well-meaning and kingdom-motivated, we've leveraged Jesus's sacrifice to satisfy our priorities and our interests.

Turns out, we weren't the only ones to make that mistake. After Jesus told the disciples about his impending death, they were in distress. However, that didn't stop them debating amongst themselves about their own egos and interests. Matthew reports that the disciples asked Jesus this question: "Who is the greatest in the Kingdom of Heaven?" (Matthew 18:1). Now, Jesus had just explained his death and that should have provided an occasion for extended reflection of their teacher's words and flawless example. Instead, they'd shifted the focus back to themselves.

Earlier I mentioned growing up with lots of miniature versions of Jesus hanging on the cross. The versions that I grew accustomed to seeing were of an emaciated Jesus tacked to a wooden cross with a strip of cloth artfully draped over his midsection to keep Jesus's crucifixion at a G-rating for family-friendly viewing at church as well as on necklaces and mass-produced artwork. While I'm not completely convinced that protecting Jesus's modesty was on the soldiers' agenda as they savagely nailed Jesus to the cross, I'm pretty sure that there would be a much smaller commercial market for a naked, beaten man on a piece of wood.

It wasn't until I came across a painting by a nineteenth-century artist that I begin to see Jesus's crucifixion from a new perspective.

In 1890, French painter James Tissot released a watercolor painting titled "Ce que voyait Notre-Seigneur sur la Croix," or "What Our Lord Saw from the Cross." Tissot did not paint that masterpiece until later in his life. He had become well-known and wealthy for his paintings of high fashion women, but during his midlife, he experienced a revival of his Catholic faith. After visiting the Middle East, he spent many years painting over 350 works of art that featured different scenes from the life of Christ. While the painting is owned by the Brooklyn Museum, it hasn't been on display since the 1930s. Art critics have several opinions of his work; however there is a renewed interest in narrative artwork and an appreciation for Tissot's paintings, even if they aren't culturally accurate (like skin color).

Unlike the traditional artistic interpretation of the crucifixion where Jesus is shown in full display on the cross in various states of agony, Tissot takes a radically different approach.

Rather than a third-person point of view, Tissot paints the crucifixion from Jesus's first-person point of view. It appears that the artist uses scripture as a reference in depicting the people and even some of the objects at the scene. Since the art is from Jesus's point of view, his entire body wouldn't be visible. Tissot chose to only include a small portion of Jesus's feet. In fact, if one isn't paying attention, it's easy to completely miss Jesus's feet in the foreground of the image.

Finding Jesus in the Psalms

Tissot's painting is powerful because it's not often that we consider the crucifixion from Jesus's point of view. We've become accustomed at looking at the crucifixion from our bystander point of view, not from Jesus's point of view, which we should agree is much more important than ours.

When we see the crucifixion from our point of view, we apply our perspective and center the emotions and reactions around how it makes us feel. Somehow, Jesus's suffering for our salvation gets lost in the translation of our fear of suffering, which leads to desire to avoid suffering or avoid those who are suffering.

How could considering Jesus's point of view during his crucifixion change your understanding of the event? It's one thing to be in tune with how you feel and what you see, but have you ever taken the time to deeply consider how Jesus may have felt as he was looking out from the cross or to really understand who and what he saw?

The phrase "holding space" describes the subtle but active posture of being present with someone in whatever condition he or she is in. To hold space well means that the space holder releases any agenda to say, do, or instruct. Likewise, the space holder suspends their timeline in favor of allowing the suffering one to just be in that space and focus on themselves while the space holder observes, supports, and empathizes.

What would it look like for you to hold space as we walk through Psalm 22? In an ideal world, a tangible equivalent would be to spend the amount of time from Jesus's anguished prayer of surrender through his death in a posture of reflection and observation. Whatever that duration of time, it would be quite a powerful experience. Yet, what if, on a more practical level, there was a willingness to linger, unrushed, as we investigate David's writings in Psalm 22? There's much pain and suffering in what follows, but not without great hope for us to cling to today!

As David writes and we see the relationship from his words to the experience of Jesus, challenge yourself to read from the perspective of Jesus on the cross rather than reading as though you are watching Jesus on the cross. See if that subtle but powerful shift magnifies your connection and your curiosity as well as provides a transformative appreciation of all that Jesus went through for you.

My God!

Psalm 22 opens with words that sound hauntingly familiar: "My God, my God, why have you abandoned me?"

David wrote these words as expression of his inner despair, but at the same time, he pens the expressed anguish of all humanity. Those nine words have been recycled an infinitesimal number of times on sick beds, by gravesides, and in the silence of unanswered prayers or the countless moments when our faces are on the ground and our hearts are destroyed. Perhaps even now, you silently rage those words at God wondering, waiting, or worrying that maybe He's fed up or had enough with you.

At the pivotal moment in human history, Jesus chose David's words to express the depth of his despair: "At about three o'clock, Jesus called out with a loud voice, '*Eli, Eli, lema sabachthani?*' which means 'My God, my God, why have you abandoned me?'"

Jesus knew the scriptures. He knew David's words, and, in that moment, Jesus spoke the divinely inspired words written long ago as his heart cry.

Jesus hung on the cross for six hours. That's a long time to hang in pain. I wonder what was worse for Jesus, the physical pain or mental pain? Did Jesus have distressing flashbacks of his beating or watching his disciples scatter when he was arrested? Imagine Tissot's painting and put yourself in Jesus's place as he looks out on the jeering crowd and the fearful, painful looks on his mother and disciple's faces. Finally, visualize yourself looking up from the cross at heaven. While knowing God's great plan for our salvation, did Jesus's eyes sweep the skies looking for any kind of shifting clouds or spark in the heaven that his desperate question was heard?

As I ponder this moment, I remember that Jesus is intimately acquainted with our pain, both physically and emotionally. Jesus knows the anguish of bearing pain alone and without relief. If this is you, Jesus understands. You are seen in whatever circumstance or past that feels like it has crucified your tender soul.

Jesus was crucified at Golgotha, which seemed to be a highly trafficked area where people could pass by or stop and watch. Not only that, but atop the cross was a *titulus,* or a sign that identified Jesus and his crimes.[1] Scholars note that each Gospel lists slightly different language, suggesting that this indictment was written in Hebrew, Greek, and Latin.[2] A few verses before Jesus calls out, the scriptural author Matthew reports that around noon, darkness descended until around 3 p.m. and then Jesus cries out to God. Could this have been the moment when the full weight of humanity's sin from the garden of Eden through the unassigned time in the future settles on Jesus's shoulders?

Even though Jesus speaks David's words from the torture of the cross, scholars and commentators can't point with certainty to an event or circumstance in David's life that would have evoked the despair expressed in these words.

Consider the plea that David cries out in Psalm 22:1 and Jesus in Matthew 27:46. Both call out "my God," not once but twice. Using the personal pronoun "my" lets us know that they not only tapped into their personal connection with God, but also believed that God would hear their desperation.

One of the hallmarks of our personal relationship with God rests in knowing that he hears us when we cry. After all, the scriptures beckon us to address God as our Abba Father. Depending on the quality of your relationship or lack of relationship with your father, the concept of God as a loving Abba may be a stretch for you. Perhaps you know what it feels like to call out for your father and only hear silence. Jesus understands.

When God doesn't seem responsive or feels distant, that sense of abandonment cuts us to the core. It's one thing for a repair person to be a no-show or an online dating connection to ghost you, but the silence or abandonment of someone who promised to love and care causes us to question our value or worth as humans.

The cross has been a symbol of hope for us that God hasn't forgotten us.

In 2014, *USA Today* interviewed a between-jobs union laborer who called his discovery after the September 11 attacks a "heavenly symbol in a hellish setting." While he'd only been working for two days at Ground Zero, Frank Sileccia was understandably traumatized and overwhelmed. During the interview, Sileccia explained that he had just helped pull two bodies from the devastating scene when he noticed a seventeen-foot section of intersecting metal beams that was shaped like a cross. Noticing that cross touched him. "It was a sign that God hadn't deserted us."[3]

That cross cut through deep despair and was a symbol of hope.

Additionally, a pastor who prayed and counseled with first responders at Ground Zero during the early days after the national tragedy recalled a conversation with a firefighter who found great comfort in that cross. The firefighter told him, "When I saw the cross, I had hope. When I saw the cross, I felt comfort." The pastor pondered why that cross brought the firefighter hope in such a hellish situation? This was the pastor's answer: "Because Jesus understands suffering. The death of Jesus Christ isn't the end of the story. It's the theme of the story."[4]

Can you put yourself in Jesus's place on the cross and imagine the ache in his heart as he remembered all of the times when he went to lonely places to pray and converse with God, but then as he hung on the cross, heaven felt silent. Jesus resided in heaven before coming to earth, he never sinned, and yet, on that cross, he was forsaken. But not because God turned his back on Jesus, but because in that moment, Jesus was completely covered in the death stench of humanity's sin.

While Jesus was fully God, he walked among humanity and shared our experience. He came to earth to show us what God was really like, but he surrendered his heavenly status in order to become like us.

> **While Jesus was fully God, he walked among humanity and shared our experience. He came to earth to show us what God was really like, but he surrendered his heavenly status in order to become like us.**

In the latter portion of Psalm 22:1, David continues to question God and Jesus's cries reflect the same question. He asks the "why God" question and the "aren't you going to save me" question. Even as Jesus wears the death cloak of our sin, his cries sound familiar to our human ears.

We've all asked the "why" question. In my reflection of my life as well as observing other believers during my tenure as a pastor, life-coach, and now speaker and author, I've noticed that the "why God" question is motivated by pain rather than reason. As my family was tossed along the rough waters of an addiction crisis on the sinking piece of driftwood that was my marriage, I cried out "why God" repeatedly. I was desperate for my God to pluck me from the jaws of the pain that gnawed off pieces of my heart each day. In *Shattered Dreams*, best-selling author and psychologist Dr. Larry Crabb expresses a candid observation that sums up our painful frustration with God: "God didn't do what I thought a good friend would do, especially a friend with a lot of resources to do a lot."[5]

Perhaps you're asking the "why God" question because you hope that the answer will curb your gutted grief or give you the closure that you need to move on. No matter the reason, we ask the question, like David and Jesus. The answer isn't as easy, is it?

Confidence in Re-Membering
(Psalms 22:3)

After crying out in anguish to God, David remembers: "Yet you are holy, / enthroned on the praises of Israel" (Psalm 22:3).

In the New Living Translation, the first word in Psalm 22:3 is "yet." It's a word that flickers with a flash of hope. Even in his anguished mindset, David transitions into a reflection from his place of deep suffering that will steal victory out of the jaws of despair that seem guaranteed to defeat. While David writes of his anguish, it's not the only story that David tells himself. David doesn't let his pain hijack his perspective.

It's a courageous act of faith to keep God's power and sovereignty foremost in our minds rather than our personal pain or difficult experiences. Trusting God doesn't take away our pain, but trusting God is like being carried in a protective boat that will guide us through our pain toward God's goodness.

David voices God's holiness and the importance of remembering that God is not like us. Scriptural authors before David expressed similar sentiments in hard times:

> "My thoughts are nothing like your thoughts," says the LORD.
> "And my ways are far beyond anything you could imagine.
> For just as the heavens are higher than the earth,
>   so my ways are higher than your ways
>   and my thoughts higher than your thoughts."
>
> (Isaiah 55:8-9)

When David writes in Psalm 22:1 that God is holy, he's saying that among many other things that God doesn't operate like us. God's sovereign plans are perfection and accomplish purposes and he holds the power to pull it off. Ask yourself this question: Given an option between your personal agenda and God's plan, which one has the best chance of blessing you in the long run even if you've got to bear some painful crosses along the way?

In *The Broken Way*, Ann Voscamp proposes that it is our remembering God and his faithfulness that helps put ourselves in position for God's healing in the face of heartache.

> I wonder if all of the bad brokenness in the world begins with the act of forgetting—forgetting God is enough, forgetting what He gives is good enough...
>
> That is why we're called to be the re-membering people—remembering the heart of God for us, remembering the cross and the communion and the crucifixion...remembering to be broken and given into the world—so Jesus can re-member all our broken hearts.[6]

In the face of great pain, we don't know what will happen in the future, so one of our most powerful spiritual analgesics is dosing ourselves with memories of God's past love and care toward us and others.

As Jesus hung on the cross, his gut-wrenching question, "My God, why have you forsaken me?" may have seemed like the end of a tragic story. As God heard those words, the Father's heart had to have broken in that moment.

Not Forgetting God's Faithfulness (Psalm 22:4)

> *Our ancestors trusted in you,*
> *and you rescued them.*
> *(Psalm 22:4)*

As David talks in Psalm 22:4 of how the ancestors trusted in God, I must admit that I initially thought, "Are you sure about that?"

The Old Testament narrative is filled with stories of failures and lack of faithfulness to God, but there were shining moments when men and women of God displayed great faith that inspire and instruct us today (Romans 15:4). Just as we've taken the time to look at the crucifixion from Jesus's perspective, we can also zoom out and look at the great men and women of faith that David refers to from God's perspective.

At various points in the Old Testament, the Israelites would gather and listen to the long history of God's faithfulness in their story. In one instance, Moses gathered the Israelites before entering the Promised Land. While their parents had died in the wilderness because of their rebellion against God (Numbers 13–14), Moses spoke to the new generation of Israelites as if they were the ones who'd been around during their 40-year odyssey in the desert. Moses uses "you" and "we" as a point of view, ostensibly to make sure that this younger audience knew that they were connected by blood to their parents and Hebrew community as well as connected by covenant to God (Deuteronomy 2).

As David writes in Psalms about God's faithfulness in freeing the Israelites from their enemies and physical captivity in the past, we celebrate the greater freedom that God would make possible in the future through Christ.

When Paul wrote to the Galatians about the gospel, he reminded them Jesus came to set them free and warned them not to believe or behave in a way that would lead them back into slavery (Galatians 5:1). This time, Paul wasn't talking about bondage to a foreign king, rather getting trapped in the shackles of religious rules that promise righteousness, but never deliver.

While David fought to keep the Israelites free from rival kings and rebellion from within his own ranks, he also knew the pressures of following God's laws. Whether it was performing the sacrifices or observing certain rules, the Israelites didn't experience the freedom that comes with the gift of grace that we enjoy today. But it's a gift that didn't come without sacrifice.

Feeling Low and Hanging High (Psalm 22:6-8)

If you're ever talking to a friend and they describe their current vibe as feeling like a worm, it's a solid clue that life could be better. I applaud David's vulnerability and candor as he describes his current self-image and how others are treating him: "But I am a worm and not a man. / I am scorned and despised by all!" (Psalm 22:6).

I'm not sure that a worm is the kind of animal that can ever live its best life. As humans, we're not taking heroic measures not to step on the worm on the sidewalk. God created worms, so he stamped his approval of "good" on them. Worms play a helpful role in soil health, which is important for our food supply. However, in biblical imagery, the reference to a worm is a symbol of weakness and lament.[7] This isn't the social media, forward-facing depiction that we'd associate with David. Even before he was king, David possessed a confident, military prowess, so describing himself as a worm must have been related to an intense inner struggle that must have stripped him clean and laid him low.

The rest of David's lament, or anguished explanation, reflects Isaiah's prophesy about how Jesus would be despised and rejected by others (Isaiah 53:3). As Jesus hung on the cross, the prophetic words of Psalm 22:7-8 are fulfilled:

> Everyone who sees me mocks me.
>   They sneer and shake their heads, saying,
> "Is this the one who relies on the LORD?
>   Then let the LORD save him!
> If the LORD loves him so much,
>   let the LORD rescue him!"
>
> (Psalm 22:7-8)

Matthew's account records how the chief priests and others looked at Jesus and mocked him for not saving himself:

Finding Jesus as Our Savior

> *He saved others... but he can't save himself! So he is the King of Israel, is he? Let him come down from the cross right now, and we will believe in him!*
>
> *(Matthew 27:42)*

Consider the scene from Jesus's perspective. He's gasping in physical pain, his body not able to process the agony of trying to breathe, the raw wood rubbing against his shredded flesh, and the spikes in his hands and feet splitting the holes in his skin even further. Yet, as Jesus hangs in physical anguish, his heart must have hurt from an overload of emotional and mental pain. The crowd looks at Jesus like motorists slowing to stare at a horrible car accident. They gawk to satisfy their own self-interest without giving a second thought to the suffering. Jesus heard the insults and mocking words as his blood drips from his body down to the ground. His blood is soaked with the stench of their sin and ours.

As you linger on this moment, from Jesus's perspective, what else do you see or feel?

At the end of Psalm 22:8, David writes "If the LORD loves him so much, / let the LORD rescue him." Again, this is the prophetic word fulfilled when religious leaders questioned why Jesus didn't just call for God to save him. It's also eerily like Satan's temptation of Jesus before his public ministry began. I wonder if Jesus thought back to the time when he could have avoided the cross?

Prior to the start of Jesus's earthly ministry, he spent forty days in the wilderness where Satan tempted him to use Jesus's divine nature to satisfy his human desires. During one temptation, Satan took Jesus to the top of Herod's temple and invited Jesus to jump off. Satan misquotes Psalm 91:3 and warps scripture to create a rationale God would send angels to protect Jesus from harm. Jesus quotes from Deuteronomy 6:16 about not testing God.

As Jesus stood atop that temple, I wonder if part of the temptation that he grappled with was the temptation to save people through a spectacular scene like jumping off a building and having the crowd watch angels miraculously save him rather than having to endure becoming a bloody sacrifice?

But God had other plans that looked bad for a few moments, yet were for our eternal good:

> But it was the LORD's good plan to crush him
>   and cause him grief.
> Yet when his life is made an offering for sin,
>   he will have many descendants.
> He will enjoy a long life,
>   and the Lord's good plan will prosper in his hands.
>   (Isaiah 53:10)

God's good plan for Jesus as well as humanity doesn't always seem good to us. But, it's not God's plan that is bad; it's the sin in our world and God's enemies who try to disrupt God's plan that warp our understanding of God's plan. Not only that, but a plan means that there is a process. We should be careful to judge a plan before the process is complete. Just as you wouldn't look into the oven at a half-baked cake and call it a failure, we shouldn't look at our lives or circumstances at the low points or disappointing moments and conclude that God has let us down.

In David's life and Jesus's resurrection, God's good plan prevailed. May this give you hope that God's good plan will prevail in your life as you trust him. He does have a plan that is for your good, even if it doesn't look good right now. Keep trusting God and he will guide you to a hope and a life-giving purpose and a lasting legacy that is far beyond anything that you could ever ask or imagine.

Enemies Closing In
(Psalm 22:11-18)

As David continues to write, he shifts to the trouble surrounding him. This couldn't have been easy given the expression of his emotional state. Certain verses of this psalm may prompt you to question whether David fears an execution, which is the exact reality that Jesus faced at the cross.

> *My enemies surround me like a herd of bulls;*
> *   fierce bulls of Bashan have hemmed me in!*
> *Like lions they open their jaws against me,*
> *   roaring and tearing into their prey.*
>
> *(Psalm 22:12-13)*

He describes vicious animals as metaphors to depict the mortal danger that he's in. It seems as if there's a play to kill him. The wild bulls of Bashan isolate their prey and circle it before attacking. Now, I've never seen wild bulls attack in person—and I'm okay with never having that experience—but it doesn't take a lot of imagination to figure out that whatever the prey, it's going to be ripped, mangled, and devoured.

His graphic description leaves little to the imagination. David doesn't tease like he's in a little danger; he's got killing trouble. He writes of physical torture that is akin to an execution, like Jesus's crucifixion.

Consider all who were responsible for condemning Jesus including the Pharisees, Sadducees, Romans, centurions, and regular people, albeit ancient people, screaming that Jesus should be crucified instead of a notorious criminal named Barabbas (Matthew 27:20). They surrounded Jesus with their plots, lies, and eventually with their condemnation, whips, and cross. There were many points in Jesus's public ministry when Jesus was supernaturally removed from peril, whether he was removed by God's Spirit or by some other means, but not this time.

David writes an incredibly knowledgeable record of what happens during Jesus's crucifixion, from the piercing of his hands and feet to the prophecy. He also writes this in Psalm 22:17: "I can count all my bones."

A few verses earlier, David writes that his bones were out of joint. That sounds painful and uncomfortable, but at least they weren't broken. That's positive, right? Yet, David's words are fulfilled in Jesus's crucifixion. In Psalm 34:20, David writes that the Messiah's bones will remain unbroken, tying back to when God instituted the Passover while the Israelites were still in Egypt, he instructed them to choose a lamb, but not break any of its bones (Exodus 12:46). It was custom for Roman soldiers to break the bones of those crucified but still alive. Breaking their legs would prevent them from pushing up their body to keep the flow of oxygen, therefore speeding up their inevitable death.[8] However, Jesus had died by the time the soldiers came around, so they didn't break his bones, and in doing so, they unknowingly fulfilled the prophecy.

Right before David moves back into a positive posture, he notes that his clothes have been taken and essentially put on eBay for the highest bidder, or more accurately, dice roller. I don't know about you, but I can't quite wrap my mind around King David being in the kind of position where others are tossing the dice to claim his royal garments. Again, since there isn't a specific time in David's life identified in the psalm, his words could be purely prophetic, but I also wonder if also metaphoric. Clothes can convey status and King David's priestly garments would have been quite desirable. Perhaps his words about dividing his garments could be a metaphor for how his sons jockeyed for his royal throne? Regardless of what was happening in his life, David's words were fulfilled in Matthew 27:35 when it was reported that after Jesus was crucified, his clothes were divided and gambled away.

As we end this section, it's not looking good. Yet, David's tone is about to shift from desperation to invitation. He's about to show us what it looks like to call out to God for help and to praise God, even from the low places in life.

God, "You Are My Strength"
(Psalms 22:19-21)

For much of my early Christian life, I admired the people around me who could boldly cry out to Jesus. These were the people who had no problem coming down to the altar call on a Sunday morning crying "Help me, Lord." Their willingness to admit their need openly inspired yet intimidated me. For so long, I wondered if God was bothered by my neediness. As one who found great comfort in following restrictive religious rules, I liked the idea that if I was good enough, then I wouldn't get myself in situations requiring that I come to God like a failure or a beggar. In my mind, God liked me better if I was low maintenance.

As I journeyed through high-level drama, I discovered that God loved it when I showed up before his throne of mercy in dire straits. While God was close to me in my struggle, his blessing was showing me the depth of his love and grace in situations that sin and selfish motivations created, but his Spirit could supernaturally redeem.

You can see in the following verse that David seemed to have already a sense of God's love for him. David spends a few verses before God crying out with big, specific prayer requests.

Psalm 22:19 should look familiar: "O Lord, do not stay far away! / You are my strength; come quickly to my aid!"

David called out a similar prayer in verse 11. This encourages me to remember that it's okay to keep calling out to God, especially when life is intense. However, when David calls out for God for help, he says it's because trouble is near. However, in Psalm 22:19, David doesn't want God to get too far away because he needs his strength and saving power.

There are times when we call on God because our eyes are on our problems and then other times that we call on God because our eyes are on him.

This is a subtle, but game-changing lesson for all of us. There are times when we call on God because our eyes are on our problems and then other times that we call on God because our eyes are on him. It's so valuable to recognize those moments in our lives. When we call on God because we're terrified of our troubles, our thoughts are split between our fears and our faith. Yet, when we focus and call on God while looking toward him, this is where we find peace and security. We have peace because we remember God's faithfulness in our past and that gives us confidence and security as we deal with the unknown future.

Next, David asks for God to "save him from the sword." David recognized that he did not have the ability to save himself. David isn't questioning whether God can save him, rather he is confident that God will. I also appreciate that David affirms that his life is worth saving: "Save me from the sword; / spare my precious life from these dogs" (Psalm 22:20).

This short verse feels like a whole lesson in grace, God's undeserved favor toward us. The whole reason that Jesus hung on that cross was because you and I have an eternal death sentence that we can't save ourselves from. Yet, our lives are precious to God, so that is why he sent Jesus to save us.

Your life matters to God so much! I've had countless conversations with people over the years who believed that they were too far gone for God to save. People who supposed that they'd sinned far too often, drunk far too much, lied far too often, or hurt others beyond repair. Yet, the message of the Bible is the same for every single one of us: Jesus saves. We are saved because God wanted to send Jesus to save us. Period.

While we can't know the reason that everything happens, I believe that there are no coincidental opportunities. So, maybe you need some encouragement today to cry to God like David. Here is your chance. Rather than focusing on whatever is in front of you that is big, scary, or seems unforgivable, challenge yourself to ten courageous seconds of calling out to God and asking him to save you from whatever has been chasing you and trying to take you down—whether it's a negative attitude, a painful past, a hidden mistake or regret, or even a crippling fear—call out to God for him to save you today.

Celebrating God with Praise and Honor (Psalm 22:23-28)

How glorious it is that we get to celebrate Resurrection Sunday once a year! It's the Sunday that we prepare for in advance, whether it's buying new spring outfits, making plans for a special dinner, selecting special songs for church, or making plans to actually make it to church. Easter Sunday is special. However, what makes Easter special is when we center our attention on celebrating and praising God.

David's praises in the later portion of Psalm 22 don't appear to be connected to a special event or occasion. He's writing and encouraging others to praise God simply because God is worthy of praise.

Here's David's declaration in Psalm 22:22-23:

I will proclaim your name to my brothers and sisters.
I will praise you among your assembled people.
*Praise the L*ORD*, all you who fear him!*
Honor him, all you descendants of Jacob!
Show him reverence, all you descendants of Israel!

The man after God's own heart as well as the man who made monumental mistakes on many occasions gives us a master class on how he intends to praise God. He's ready to celebrate God in front of God's people. He wants to stand up publicly to his Israelite brothers and sisters with praises to God.

Not only that, but in verse 23, David tells his audience that they need to praise God as well.

While *praise* is a churchy word that people interpret a lot of different ways, it come down to celebrating and elevating. The word *praise* seems less loaded if someone lavishes it on the Broadway performance or their favorite sports team. However, when it comes to God, there's a tendency to get shy and reserved with our praise. Perhaps, David sensed this as well, hence his emphatic command for all those who follow God to praise him.

Let's consider ourselves to be in the crowd of people that David is calling to praise God. If it's been a minute since you've stopped to praise God intentionally, or perhaps you've gotten a wrong picture in your head of what you need to say, I've got some helpful phrases here that we'll call "Praise Phrases 101":

- "I worship you alone, God."
- "There is no one like you, God."
- "You alone are God Almighty."
- "Thank you for blessing me."

Praising God isn't about waiting for a certain emotion to overtake you or even feeling like doing it. Celebrating God and elevating his name happens when your head and heart come into agreement, and you express that agreement in phrases like those I've given in the examples above. Best of all, offering praise to God isn't just for a specific time frame when you're standing in church. I tend to praise God when my eyes open in the morning. Not because I'm a morning person but because when my eyes open each morning, I'm reminded that even the pure act of opening my eyes is an act of God's sovereign grace that is worthy of celebrating.

No one can force you to praise God if your heart isn't in it, but then, you'll need to ask the question, "Why isn't my heart in it?" Do you have a praise hiccup either in your heart or mind that makes it hard to declare those phrases of praise? Sometimes, when we're disappointed with God, it can impact our desire to offer praise. Other possibilities include not feeling close to God, guilt, shame, or indifference. But David also gives us a clue to the kind of person who is mostly likely to praise God in verse 26 and how praising God will impact their attitude: "All who seek the LORD will praise him. / Their hearts will rejoice with everlasting joy" (Psalm 22:26b).

Is it me or based on David's words does it seem like intentionally praising God leads to a joyful heart? That's sounds like a pretty good deal, unless you are a fan of negativity, guilt, or shame. When we take the focus off ourselves and fixate on our glorious

God, that yields a mental, emotional, spiritual, and arguably a physical boon for our quality of life. Even more, our praise to God and subsequent joy becomes an attractive magnet that draws in an unbelieving world. There's a progression to God's plan beyond the cross that we play a part in: "The whole earth will acknowledge the LORD and return to him. / All the families of the nations will bow down before him" (Psalm 22:27).

The takeaway is that when you praise God, elevating his name above the other good priorities in your life, whether it's career, a healthy retirement, or your golf-handicap, the unbelievers around you notice. As they notice your increasing joy, especially in a world where negativity and pain are so common, they'll get curious about how they can experience what you've received from God. Your praise can lay the path for others to find their hope in Christ!

Leaving Your Legacy of Praise (Psalm 22:29-30)

As Psalm 22 ends, David casts a vision for the future generations. He proclaims that not only will the children of God's people serve him, but that the stories of God will be shared with future generations, even those who aren't born yet.

> *Our children will also serve him.*
> *Future generations will hear about the wonders of the Lord.*
> *His righteous acts will be told to those not yet born.*
> *They will hear about everything he has done.*
> *(Psalm 22:30-31)*

We're that future generation and we are also the ones who will share with the next future generation. Consider this: Each time we share our stories and openly praise God faithfully for what he has done through Christ in our lives, each act lays a path for future generations to follow. We know that this isn't a guarantee that your children, nieces, nephews, or grandchildren will choose Christ for themselves, but shouldn't we give them the opportunity to hear God's great gospel work in our lives? For sure, they will face the same, if not greater challenges than we have, so let's give them a road map to hope by allowing them to hear and see our praise of God, not just on Easter Sunday, but every day.

When David writes that future generations will be told and will hear everything he has done, who will do the telling? I'm raising my hand for that job right now, even if the future generation doesn't always seem to be listening. You get to decide whether that will be you.

CONCLUSION

Thank you for joining me on this adventure of finding Jesus in the Psalms. As I mentioned at the beginning of our Lenten journey toward the cross, there's a security and confidence in knowing that God planned for our salvation, peace, and eternal future long ago. Like a parent who starts a college savings fund for their child at birth, God invested in your spiritual future by determining long ago that Jesus would give his life as the perfect sacrifice. As you read through the Old Testament, especially the Psalms, you can see the shadowy footprint of Jesus's own journey centuries before he came to earth to walk among us to show us what God was like.

I also hope that you enjoyed learning more about King David, who offered an early glimpse of what a prophet-priest-king would be like. While imperfect in many ways, David demonstrates love and commitment to God as well as a humble heart and hopeful attitude. Studying David's life during this experience has reminded me that God isn't looking for me to be perfect, rather God desires that I trust in his promises for my life and his Big Picture plan for humanity. I pray that you embrace those lessons as well.

Whenever I conclude a Bible study project, I like to end our time together with a prayer for you. This blessing captures some of the big ideas that we've explored together and the faith lessons that I hope will stay with you in the months and years to come.

Final Prayer of Celebration

God, thank you for walking with us through Lent as we've explored Jesus in the Psalms. As we've gotten to know you and your Big Picture for humanity even more, we praise you for the new discoveries, understandings, and revelations that we've gained through this experience. I pray that in the days ahead, we would continue to allow your Spirit to keep teaching us.

We thank you that Jesus is with us in hard places so that we will remember that we do not need to fear tough times or personal struggle.

We thank you that Jesus is our Good Shepherd and that we will live confidently that he will lead us to peace, purpose, and joy in our lives.

We thank you that Jesus is our hope so we already celebrate our victory in this life and beyond.

We thank you that Jesus is our strength for each day, so we can be strong and courageous when facing any circumstance and expect that you will provide every need.

Finally, God, we thank you that Jesus is our Savior and for the gift of our salvation, and we will live in the freedom that he died to bring us.

Thank you, God, for the enduring truth of your promises and your lavish love and grace. May we choose to walk each day in the light of Jesus's sacrifice and shine that light through our lives and legacy so that others may also discover the hope of Christ.

Notes

Chapter 1

1. Stephen Burt, "Why People Need Poetry," https://www.youtube.com/watch?v=08ZWROqoTZ0 , accessed June 5, 2022, (time stamp: 1:32).
2. E. Ray Clendenen and Jeremy Royal Howard, eds., *Holman Illustrated Bible Commentary* (Nashville: B&H Publishing Group, 2015), 545.
3. Warren W. Wiersbe, *The Wiersbe Bible Commentary: Old Testament* (Colorado Springs, CO: David C. Cook, 2007), 870.
4. Matthew 9:27, Matthew 12:23, Matthew 15:22, Matthew 20:30, Matthew 21:9
5. David Guzik, "Psalm 132—Remembering the Promise to David and Beyond," https://enduringword.com/bible-commentary/psalm-132/amp/, accessed April 28, 2022.
6. Bible Project, "Overview: Psalms," https://www.youtube.com/watch?v=j9phNEaPrv8, accessed April 18, 2022.
7. John Ortberg. *God Is Closer Than You Think* (Grand Rapids: Zondervan, 2005), 13.
8. Leland Melvin, *Chasing Space: An Astronaut's Story of Grit, Grace, and Second Chances* (New York: Amistad/HarperCollins, 2017), 151.
9. Clendenden and Howard, *Holman Illustrated Bible Commentary*, 547.
10. "Ellicott's Commentary for English Readers," s.v. Psalm 2, https://biblehub.com/commentaries/ellicott/psalms/2.htm, accessed June 6, 2022.
11. National Religious Broadcasters, "H. B. Charles Preaches on Psalm 2 at NRB's Proclaim 19 Convention," https://www.youtube.com/watch?v=g0Y_QxFrfkg, accessed June 6, 2022, (time stamp: 9:45).
12. Mark Galli, "Persecution in the Early Church: A Gallery of Persecuting Emperors," https://christianhistoryinstitute.org/magazine/article/persecution-in-early-church-gallery, accessed June 6, 2022.
13. Wiersbe, *The Wiersbe Bible Commentary: Old Testament*, 874.

Notes

Chapter 2

1. https://www.blueletterbible.org/study/parallel/paral18.cfm, accessed June 7, 2022.
2. Wiersbe, *The Wiersbe Bible Commentary: Old Testament*, 891.
3. Bible Hub, s.v. "towb," https://biblehub.com/hebrew/2896.htm, accessed May 20, 2022.
4. R. C. Sproul, *The Holiness of God*, rev. ed. (Carol Stream, IL: Tyndale, 1988).
5. C. S. Lewis, *A Mind Awake: An Anthology of C. S. Lewis*, edited by Clyde Kilby (Harvest Books/Harcourt, Brace and Company, 2003), 75.
6. Bible Hub, s.v. "Shoel," https://biblehub.com/hebrew/7585.htm, accessed May 15, 2022.
7. Will Davis Jr., *10 Things Jesus Never Said: And Why You Should Stop Believing Them* (Grand Rapids, MI: Revell, 2011), 150.

Chapter 3

1. Bhvishya Patel, "Boy Rescues Lamb Trapped in Drainage Ditch… Only For It to Leap Straight Back In," https://www.dailymail.co.uk/news/article-9511557/amp/Boy-rescues-lamb-trapped-drainage-ditch-leap-straight-in.html, April 26, 2021.
2. Bible Hub, "Benson Commentary," s.v. "Ezekiel," https://biblehub.com/commentaries/benson/ezekiel/34.htm, accessed June 9, 2022.
3. David Guzik, "Psalm 23—The Lord Is My Shepherd and My Host," https://enduringword.com/bible-commentary/psalm-23/, accessed June 15, 2022.
4. Ronald F. Youngblood, *Nelson's Illustrated Bible Dictionary: New and Enhanced Edition* (Nashville: Thomas Nelson, 2014), 66.
5. W. Phillip Keller, *A Shepherd Looks at Psalm 23* (Grand Rapids, MI: Zondervan, 2008), 24.
6. Lysa TerKeurst, *Finding I AM: How Jesus Fully Satisfies the Cry of Your Heart* (Nashville: Lifeway Press, 2017), 125.

Chapter 4

1. "The Holy Spirit in the Old Testament," https://www.thomasnelsonbibles.com/blog/the-holy-spirit-in-the-old-testament/.
2. Got Questions Ministries, "How and When Was the Canon of the Bible Put Together," https://www.gotquestions.org/canon-Bible.html.
3. Wiersbe, *The Wiersbe Bible Commentary: Old Testament*, 995.
4. Bible Hub, s.v. "elohim," https://biblehub.com/hebrew/430.htm.
5. Bible Hub, s.v. "Yhvh," https://biblehub.com/hebrew/3068.htm.
6. Youngblood, *Nelson's Illustrated Bible Dictionary*, 1201.
7. Bible Hub, s.v. "kurios," https://biblehub.com/greek/2962.htm.
8. Britannica, "Yahweh," https://www.britannica.com/topic/Yahweh.
9. Bible Hub, s.v. "ladoni," https://www.biblehub.com/hebrew/ladoni_113.htm.
10. Al Garza, "Is Jesus God in Psalm 110:1 Debate," https://youtu.be/lo7GEB6foIA, accessed July 25, 2022.

Notes

11 Al Garza, "Is Jesus God in Psalm 110:1 Debate, https://youtu.be/lo7GEB6foIA, accessed July 25, 2022.
12 Bible Hub, s.v. "kurios," https://biblehub.com/greek/2962.htm.
13 Mark Clark, "5 Cultural Shifts We Need to Understand to Reach the West," https://careynieuwhof.com/5-cultural-shifts-we-need-to-understand-to-reach-the-west/, accessed July 25, 2022.
14 Bible Hub, s.v. "Salem," https://biblehub.com/greek/4532.htm, accessed May 11, 2022.
15 Youngblood, *Nelson's Illustrated Bible Dictionary*, 738.
16 David Guzik, "Psalm 110—Messiah, Priest, Conquering King," https://enduringword.com/bible-commentary/psalm-110, accessed May 8, 2022.
17 Bible Hub, s.v. "Adonay," https://biblehub.com/hebrew/136.htm.

Chapter 5

1 Youngblood, *Nelson's Illustrated Bible Dictionary*, 439.
2 Youngblood, *Nelson's Illustrated Bible Dictionary*, 911.
3 Clendenden and Howard, "Matthew 26:36-38," *Holman Illustrated Bible Commentary*, 1042.
4 Wiersbe, *The Wiersbe Commentary: Old Testament*, 950.
5 George Barna, "New Insights into the Generation of Growing Influence: Millenials in America," A Research Report by George Barna, Cultural ResearchCenter at Arizona Christian University, 2021, https://www.arizonachristian.edu/wp-content/uploads/2021/10/George-Barna-Millennial-Report-2021-FINAL-Web.pdf.

Chapter 6

1 Bible Hub, "Ellicott Commentary for English Readers," s.v. Matthew 27, https://biblehub.com/commentaries/ellicott/matthew/27.htm, accessed June 14, 2022.
2 Warren W. Wiersbe, *The Wiersbe Bible Commentary: New Testament* (Colorado Springs, CO: David C. Cook, 2007), 83.
3 Rick Hampson, "Ground Zero Cross A Powerful Symbol for 9/11 Museum," *USA Today*, May 14, 2014 https://www.usatoday.com/story/news/nation/2014/05/13/911-ground-zero-museum-cross-world-trade-center/8907003/.
4 Skip Heitzig, "Cross Culture—Psalm 22—Skip Heitzig." https://youtu.be/vS9AgFaJ3rI (time stamp 3:00 and 4:40).
5 Larry Crabb, *Shattered Dreams: God's Unexpected Pathway to Joy* (Colorado Springs, CO: WaterBrook Press, 2001), 20.
6 Ann Voscamp, *The Broken Way: A Daring Path Into the Abundant Life* (Grand Rapids, MI: Zondervan, 2016), 49.
7 Youngblood, *Nelson's Illustrated Bible Dictionary*, 70.
8 Wiersbe, *The Wiersbe Commentary: New Testament*, 308.

**Watch videos based on
*Finding Jesus in the Psalms:
A Lenten Journey*
with Barb Roose
through Amplify Media.**

Amplify Media is a multimedia platform that delivers high quality, searchable content with an emphasis on Wesleyan perspectives for churchwide, group, or individual use on any device at any time. In a world of sometimes overwhelming choices, Amplify gives church leaders and congregants media capabilities that are contemporary, relevant, effective, and, most importantly, affordable and sustainable.

With **Amplify Media** church leaders can:

- Provide a reliable source of Christian content through a Wesleyan lens for teaching, training, and inspiration in a customizable library
- Deliver their own preaching and worship content in a way the congregation knows and appreciates
- Build the church's capacity to innovate with engaging content and accessible technology
- Equip the congregation to better understand the Bible and its application
- Deepen discipleship beyond the church walls

Ask your group leader or pastor about Amplify Media and sign up today at www.AmplifyMedia.com.

CPSIA information can be obtained
at www.ICGtesting.com
Printed in the USA
LVHW091754211122
733248LV00002BA/6